HISTORIC HOMES
OF AMERICA

HISTORIC HOMES
OF AMERICA

James Tackach

Portland House

A Division of Crown Publishers, Inc.

(Endpapers) Wallpaper from the home of
Charles M. Russell (see pp. 180-182)

(Previous pages) The richly detailed
Marble Hall at Whitehall, Henry M.
Flagler's estate in Palm Beach, Florida.
(see pp. 88-91)

Copyright©1990 Moore & Moore Publishing
All rights reserved.

This 1990 edition was published by Portland
House, a division of dilithium Press, Ltd.,
distributed by Crown Publishers Inc.
225 Park Avenue South
New York, New York 10003

h g f e d c b a

ISBN 0 517 69476 X

Printed and bound in Hong Kong

Historic Homes of America was prepared and
produced by Moore & Moore Publishing,
11 W. 19th Street, New York, New York 10011

An M&M Book

Project Director & Editor Gary Fishgall

Senior Editorial Assistant Shirley Vierheller;
Editorial Assistants Lisa Pike, Ben
McLaughlin, and Grace Sullivan; *Copy
Editor* Bert N. Zelman of Publishers
Workshop Inc.

Photo Research (Portraits) Lucinda Stellini

Designer Binns & Lubin/Martin Lubin

Separations and Printing Regent Publishing
Services Ltd.

Typesetting Sharon Brant Typography

CONTENTS

The Home of Noah Webster

The Home of Walt Whitman

The Home of Helen Keller

The Home of Henry Ford

The Home of Kit Carson

Introduction

The term "American home" could almost be considered a contradiction. Many foreign observers have called Americans a restless species, constantly on the move, never settling in one place very long. Over a century ago, Alexis de Tocqueville, a French visitor, wrote, "A restless temper seems to me one of the most distinctive traits of this people. The American has no time to bind himself to anything, he grows accustomed only to change and ends by regarding it as the natural state."

Indeed the Americans are a mobile people—a collection of disenfranchised wanderers from the Old World who turned their backs on their homelands and sailed away. Once in the New World, they found plenty of room for movement, an open frontier seemingly stretching forever west. They moved, established new settlements, and moved again. Even today, after the frontier has long been conquered, Americans are still on the move—to lofty Colorado, to new jobs in the Sunbelt, out of the cities to the suburbs, back to the cities.

No wonder that so much of the New World's folklore and fiction concerns not the home but the open road. Rip van Winkle, America's first homespun hero, leaves his home and nagging wife and escapes to the hills. Huck Finn takes off on a raft. The heroes of John Steinbeck, Jack Kerouac, and Saul Bellow take to the road.

Nonetheless, the impulse to move exists side by side with an impulse to settle, to build a new civilization—"a city upon a hill." Even America's escape artists try to find a place of their own. Henry David Thoreau leaves Concord but builds a cabin at Walden Pond. Huck and Jim, the runaway slave, construct a crude hut on their river raft. Steinbeck's Joad family finds shelter in an old boxcar. Perhaps America's worship of movement is not escapism but a prolonged search for home, an impulse recounted in novels like *Look Homeward, Angel* and in popular songs like "I'll Be Home for Christmas" and "Homeward Bound."

This book celebrates the American home. Not the Cape Cods, split levels, and studio apartments in which many Americans live, but the dwellings of some of America's most famous citizens—presidents, statesmen, inventors, writers, business leaders. Through the pages that follow, we will enter the private worlds of people whom we may know only in history books; perhaps the famous will become more human when we see them in the comfort of their own homes.

But the book is not meant to be elitist; the homes range in size from Daniel Webster's four-room, single-story farmhouse to George Washington Vanderbilt's 250-room château. They also range in style from simple New England saltboxes to sprawling gingerbread Victorians. Homes from more than 30 states are represented, providing a broad geographic cross section. In age, they range from Paul Revere's 17th-century Boston dwelling to John F. Kennedy's 20th-century Brookline birthplace.

The occupants of these homes also vary greatly, though they all achieved fame. Some, like Franklin D. Roosevelt, were born into wealthy families, whereas others, like Booker T. Washington, were born as slaves. Some occupied their houses for a short time and moved on; others stayed in one home their entire lives, then passed the estates on to their children and grandchildren.

In the stories that follow, I will attempt to make some connection between dwelling and inhabitant. In some cases, that connection is easy to see; the home provides interesting insights into the life and work of its occupant—Thomas Jefferson, for example, designing Monticello as an exemplar of Palladian classic architecture adapted to the American landscape, William Faulkner trying to preserve the Old South by restoring a decaying mansion. In other cases, the relation between home and homeowner is harder to grasp. Who would guess, for example, that the first abode of Gilbert Stuart, the great portrait painter, was a snuff mill?

This book is also a tribute to those who made the effort to restore and maintain these homes. These individuals have kept alive the lives and lifestyles of some of America's most noteworthy citizens and have provided us an opportunity to learn about the time and place in which these people lived—18th-century Boston, 19th-century rural Virginia, 20th-century small-town Missouri, territorial New Mexico, and the Mecca called California. These dedicated preservationists have also given a restless people a chance to forget the road, at least for a time, and to find their way home.

(Opposite) An exterior window at Marjorie Kinnan Rawlings' home in Cross Creek, Florida provides a hint of the homey environment inside. (see pp. 114-116)

New England

As this worktable suggests, the Websters were a busy New England farm family.

NOAH WEBSTER, the man whose last name has become a synonym for "dictionary," had humble beginnings in a four-room saltbox farmhouse in the West Division of Hartford, Connecticut. Today, the house stands at 227 South Main Street, off Route 84, in West Hartford.

Noah, the fourth of Noah and Mercy Steele Webster's five children, was born on October 16, 1758. The Websters' house is a typical 18th-century Connecticut clapboard-sided farmhouse built around a large brick chimney. The lower floor holds a kitchen and what colonials called the "best room"—comparable to today's living room. It was in this room that Noah was born. The upper floor holds the bedrooms. The view from the front of the house showed Hartford in the distance; to the south was the family's 120-acre farm and the Farmington Hills.

Noah's mother was a weaver and his father was a farmer, so they needed all the help they could get from their children. Nonetheless, Noah, Sr., was an avid reader, and he made sure that his children learned to read and write. Young Noah became so enamored of books that he often stopped his work in the fields to read under a nearby tree. At first, Noah, Sr., was distressed by his son's disinterest in farmwork, but he eventually recognized the boy's potential to earn a living by other means. He encouraged young Noah to study with a local clergyman, the Reverend Nathan Perkins, and the minister began to tutor the youngster for entry into Yale College. The young man's education was interrupted by a typhoid fever epidemic and by the Revolutionary War, but he earned a degree from Yale in 1778. He studied law afterward and was admitted to the bar, but the legal profession

(Previous pages) A close-up of Noah Webster's desk.

(Opposite) This West Hartford, Connecticut, saltbox was the first home of the great lexicographer, Noah Webster.

This fireplace is located in the lean-to kitchen, built in 1787, after Noah had left the family farm.

(Opposite) The first-floor "best" room served as sleeping quarters for Mrs. Webster as well as a family room.

The attic of the Webster home has changed little in two centuries. At times, Noah's older brother slept there.

did not interest him, nor did he intend to return to the family farm.

In 1782, Webster took a teaching job at Goshen, New York, and began to write school textbooks. A year later he produced what became known as his "Blue-backed Speller," a schoolchild's primer that sold well for over a century and helped standardize American spelling. To protect his books from being copied, he proposed and lobbied for copyright laws, and as a result he is sometimes called the "father of the American copyright."

During the 1780s, Webster traveled around the country, lecturing on the need for Americans to establish a national language, distinct from its overseas roots. In 1789, his lectures were published under the title, *Dis-*

sertations on the English Language. In one essay, he urged his fellow citizens to "seize the present moment and establish a *national language* as well as a national government." During the 1790s, Webster served as the editor of two important New York Federalist newspapers, *American Minerva* and *The Herald*, and he continued to write and lecture on politics, language, and education.

In 1800, Webster announced his plans to write three new dictionaries. The last, *An American Dictionary of the English Language*, written by hand, contained more than 70,000 entries. It surpassed the contemporary edition of Samuel Johnson's dictionary in both size and scope, and it is still the prototype for today's American dictionaries.

Webster, who died in 1843 at age 85, often visited the Connecticut farmhouse, but he only lived there during a brief period in 1780 when he taught school in West Hartford. Sometime after young Noah moved out, a lean-to was added to house a new kitchen, bedroom, and pantry; and a rear ell was added years later by one of the farm's subsequent owners (Noah's parents having sold it in 1790).

Today the barn-red house is operated by the Noah Webster Foundation & Historical Society of West Hartford, Inc. Guides in colonial dress escort visitors through the house and demonstrate some of the daily chores of an 18th-century farm family.

wall, made almost entirely of glass, further suggested an outdoor court. Wall panels were enriched with onyx, marble, and bronze, and huge chandeliers were hung from the ceiling.

Off the Great Hall is the huge two-story dining room lined with gilded cornices and alabaster columns and furnished with an oak and lemonwood dining table designed to hold up to 34 guests. Other doorways off the Great Hall lead to the library, music room, morning room, billiard room, and breakfast room.

To the left of the Great Hall is a wide sweeping staircase leading to the second-floor bedrooms. Many of the rooms were designed and assembled in Europe and shipped to Newport to be installed by some of the hundreds of craftsmen and laborers who took part in the mansion's construction. The bathrooms off the bedrooms are supplied with both fresh water and salt water from the ocean. The upper floors are devoted to servants' quarters. In fact, 33 of the mansion's 70 rooms were used by the domestic staff.

Perhaps the most pleasing feature of The Breakers are the two loggias at the back of the house overlooking the wide lawn and, beyond that, the Atlantic Ocean. These open porches, which connect the building's two large wings, were furnished with wicker chairs and decorated with plants to allow for pleasant summertime lounging.

The Breakers was used by the Vanderbilts only during July and August; the rest of the year, the family lived in a much larger New York mansion. Unfortunately, Cornelius enjoyed his vacation home for only a few summers. The year after The Breakers opened, he suffered a stroke that substantially curtailed his activities. Three years later, he died at age 56.

The home stayed in the Vanderbilt family for many years, though it remained closed much of the time. In 1972, it was acquired by the Preservation Society of Newport County. The society continues to maintain The Breakers and several other Newport mansions, which are annually visited by thousands of tourists who are awed by the splendor of America's Gilded Age.

The plant-filled loggias connecting the house's two large wings, provide a splendid view of the Atlantic Ocean.

(Opposite top) The Breakers' front entranceway leads to the enormous Great Hall, 45 feet high, with a ceiling painted to represent a cloud-filled sky.

A large fireplace with a stone chimney piece imported from France warms the family library.

(Opposite bottom) Male houseguests relaxed in the billiard room, which is accented with gray-green marble and red mahogany.

WHEN PAUL REVERE bought a 90-year-old house on Boston's North Square in 1770, he surely had no idea that it would be the starting point for the most famous horseback ride in American history. The 35-year-old Revere, who would father eight children by his first wife, Sarah, and eight more by his second, Rachel, merely needed a large home to accommodate his growing family.

The house had been built in the late 1670s or early 1680s after a great fire had wiped out many of Boston's wooden buildings. It was a typical medieval-style 2½-story urban house with small windows and diamond-shaped panes. By the time Revere moved in, however, it had been expanded to three full stories. The main floor featured a large hall spanned by thick wooden beams and a kitchen in the rear with a brick oven. Upstairs were bedrooms for Revere's large family.

Revere worked as a silversmith, a trade he had learned from his father. In the mid-1770s, he also became deeply involved in the events that led to the American Revolution. He developed friendships with patriots such as Samuel Adams and John Hancock, associated with several radical groups, including the Sons of Liberty, and took part in meetings that led to the Boston Tea Party on December 16, 1773. An experienced courier, Revere became Boston's official messenger to the First Continental Congress in Philadelphia in December 1774.

But Revere is most noted for his famous ride on the night of April 18, 1775. John Hancock and Samuel Adams had left Boston to avoid British troops, and Revere was asked to ride to their Lexington quarters to warn them of their imminent arrest by soldiers en route from Boston. He first arranged with a friend to hang lanterns in the Old North Church that would advise him and other couriers of the soldiers' plans—one lantern if they were coming by land, two if they were coming by sea. Then he slipped out the rear door of his house—the square in front was crowded with Redcoats—and hurried to a carefully hidden boat to cross the Charles River and begin his ride.

At about 11 o'clock in the evening, Revere reached the opposite side of the Charles, mounted a horse, and galloped toward Lex-

Paul Revere's home, the oldest dwelling within Boston's city limits, was built in the 1670s or 1680s, after a great fire wiped out many of the city's wooden buildings.

(Opposite) The large hall on the first floor is spanned by thick wooden beams and decorated with late-17th-century furnishings. A carpet covers the small table, a common practice at the time. The press-cupboard against the wall is dated 1699.

ington, warning patriot households along the way that the British were coming by sea. At Lexington, he alerted Adams and Hancock of the impending danger and helped the two great patriots remove themselves to safety.

Throughout the war, Revere continued his involvement with the patriot cause. He served as a colonel in the Massachusetts militia. He also used his considerable artistic talents to design and produce the first Massachusetts currency and to draw the state's official seal. After the war, he continued to work as a silversmith, subsequently becoming involved in other businesses, including a hardware shop, a foundry, and a copper mill. When the famous U.S. frigate the *Constitution* (nicknamed "Old Ironsides") was built in 1797, its designers called on Revere to produce the ship's copper fittings.

Revere owned the North Square house until 1800. When he died in 1818, one obituary stated that "seldom has the tomb closed upon a life so honourable and useful."

By the mid-19th century, Revere's house

The kitchen at the rear of the house contains brick ovens and many 18th-century cooking utensils; the cradle was made from a molasses barrel.

This second-floor bedroom doubled as a parlor; the bed, chest, and clock once belonged to Revere.

had degenerated into a tenement. It was modified extensively and once was used as a store. In the early 1900s, the Paul Revere Memorial Association acquired the house and directed the painstaking task of restoration. The third story, added about the time Revere moved in, was removed (the reason for this has been lost to history). The first floor is restored to its original 17th-century condition, and the second floor is furnished as it was in Revere's time.

Today the Paul Revere House, the oldest dwelling within Boston's original city limits, is situated in a crowded neighborhood in the city's Italian section. Visitors to the house can visit nearby Paul Revere Plaza and the Old North Church a few blocks away.

One of America's great orators, Daniel Webster, was born in a humble farmhouse near Franklin, New Hampshire.

The Birthplace of
Daniel Webster
1782–1852

When my eyes shall be turned to behold for the last time the sun in heaven, may I not see him shining on the broken and dishonored fragments of a once glorious Union.

From his second speech on Foote's Resolution, January 26, 1830

Daguerreotype. c. 1841–45. Library of Congress.

THE DANIEL WEBSTER birthplace stands as testimony to the notion that great men sometimes have humble beginnings. We might expect the first home of one of America's greatest orators and senators to include a large library lined with the world's best books, but this is hardly the case.

Daniel, the fourth of five children born to Ebenezer and Abigail Eastman Webster, was born on January 18, 1782, in a small farmhouse in Franklin, New Hampshire. According to Charles Lanman, Webster's secretary and first biographer, the one-story house had a high gabled roof, a single chimney, windows on each side of the front door, and three windows on each side. Inside were four rooms and an addition in the rear, housing the kitchen. In front of the house were a well and sweep and a large elm tree. Webster lived in this house for only two years; then the family moved to a larger dwelling in nearby Salisbury.

Webster's first home suggests a family of hard-working, self-sufficient Yankee farmers, which was certainly the case. And like many other 18th-century New England families, they took religion very seriously. Mrs. Webster taught her children to read when they were very young so that they could have access to the Bible. Webster remembered his father reading passages to the family at the end of every workday and claimed that his impressive delivery "gave me a taste for the inspired authors" and the cadences of eloquent speech.

Ebenezer also read the classics, lent by a local clergyman and a local lawyer, and Daniel, who attended school irregularly, came to love the books his father brought home. The Reverend Samuel Wood noted the boy's interest and began tutoring him for Dartmouth College. Daniel indeed attended that college, graduated in 1801, and was later admitted to the New Hampshire bar.

After practicing law for more than 15 years, Daniel turned to national politics. He was elected to the House of Representatives in 1822 and to the Senate five years later. As a senator, along with Henry Clay of Kentucky and John Calhoun of South Carolina, he earned a reputation as a great orator and debater. He fiercely defended the Union at a time when its disintegration seemed imminent. Webster died in Marshfield, Massachusetts, in 1852, nine years before the start of the Civil War.

Webster's birthplace was moved or destroyed some time after the family relocated to Salisbury. But in 1904, the Webster Birthplace Association uncovered what it believed was the site of Ebenezer and Abigail's home. Local tradition maintained that part of the original Webster house had been built into the nearby Sawyer house, and that portion was used to recreate the Daniel Webster Birthplace.

IN 1873, when Harriet Beecher Stowe and her husband, Calvin, moved into a cottage on 73 Forest Street in Hartford, Connecticut, the author was already over 60 years old. She and Calvin, a noted Biblical scholar and retired professor from Bowdoin College, were looking for a fitting home where a man and woman of letters could enjoy the later years of their lives and a place where they could entertain friends and family.

Harriet was born in Litchfield, Connecticut, in 1811 and studied as a teenager at the Hartford Female Seminary. When she was 21, her father, the Reverend Lyman Beecher, moved the family to Cincinnati, Ohio where he became the president of the Lane Theological Seminary. There Harriet was first exposed to runaway slaves and their tales of misery. In 1850, 14 years after her marriage, she and her husband moved to Brunswick, Maine, where Calvin assumed a faculty position at Bowdoin College. Soon after that, Harriet began work on *Uncle Tom's Cabin*, the novel that would make her famous.

After Calvin retired, the Stowes decided to move back to Connecticut. They chose for their homesite a beautifully wooded area in Hartford known as Nook Farm. The entire tract had been bought by John Hooker and Senator Francis Gillette in 1853, and the two men sold parcels of the land to writers, other prominent individuals, and their family members. Eventually it became an enclave for the intellectual elite. Other residents included Charles Dudley Warner, an author and editor, and his wife, Susan Lee Warner, an accomplished pianist; Joseph Hawley, a former governor and senator; and, later, Mark Twain, whose house stands on Farmington Avenue (see pp. 14–16). The Stowes' first Nook Farm home, a Gothic villa called Oakholm, proved too large to maintain, so they purchased the cottage on Forest Street in 1873.

The Forest Street house had been designed and built in 1871. It was influenced by the designs of Andrew Jackson Downing and Calvert Vaux, two architects who led a Gothic revival during the early Victorian age. The three-story house features large bay windows on the first two floors, covered porches on each side of the house, and a steep hip roof. Harriet, an avid gardener, surrounded the house with her favorite plants.

Inside, the first floor comprises the sunfilled parlor at the rear of the house, an elegant dining room, and a kitchen. Harriet's bedroom

Stowe's sun-filled first-floor parlor could be used for quiet reading or for entertaining guests, like her neighbor, Mark Twain. The arched bookcases hold English and foreign editions of Stowe's works.

is on the second floor above the parlor; next door is the sitting room where she continued her literary pursuits. While at Nook Farm, she wrote several books, including *Poganuc People: Their Lives and Loves*, which makes use of her girlhood experiences in Litchfield.

Calvin died in 1886, and Harriet died 10 years later. The house was greatly remodeled and modernized during the next quarter century. In 1929, it was purchased by Harriet's grandniece, Katharine Seymour Day. When she died in 1964, she bequeathed the home to the Stowe–Day Foundation, which restored and now oversees the house and conducts tours.

In 1873, Calvin and Harriet Beecher Stowe purchased this three-story cottage in Hartford's Nook Farm district.

In this upstairs study, Harriet Beecher Stowe wrote *Poganuc People* and other works.

The Mid-Atlantic States

AMERICA'S BUSTLING, activist president, Theodore Roosevelt, is known as an outdoorsman—a hunter, horseman, hiker, and camper. His mansion on Oyster Bay in Cove Neck, Long Island, New York, is a monument to a man who loved the outdoors.

Theodore Roosevelt had known Oyster Bay as a boy because his family summered in the area. In 1883, three years after his graduation from Harvard, Roosevelt bought 155-acres near his family's vacation home for $10,000 cash and a $20,000 20-year mortgage. He kept 95 acres, sold the rest to relatives, and began making plans to build a large house on the estate for his wife, Alice, and their future family. In 1884, his wife died two days after childbirth, but Roosevelt was still determined to build a home for himself and his new daughter. He contracted a Long Island architectural firm, Lamb & Rich, to create a large mansion at the summit of his wooded Oyster Bay property. He called his estate "Sagamore Hill," after an Indian chief who once owned the land.

Roosevelt wanted a large porch "where we could sit in rocking chairs and look at the sunset." He also prescribed a library "with a shallow bay window looking south" and "big fireplaces for logs." The architects obeyed, erecting a rambling three-story Victorian frame and brick mansion with plenty of windows and more than 20 rooms. On the ground floor are the library, a large center hall, a dining room, a kitchen, a pantry and a drawing room. The second floor contains the family and guest bedrooms. The Gun Room, for Roosevelt's sizable firearm collection, occupies the third floor. Later, in 1904, Roosevelt added the first-floor North Room, which houses hunting trophies, mementos from Roosevelt's many travels, and several diplomatic gifts.

Roosevelt and his new wife, Edith, took up residence at Sagamore Hill in 1887, nearly two years after his daughter and elder sister had moved in. From here, Roosevelt began a career in public office that took him from the presidency of New York City's Police Board, to the Department of the Navy as Assistant Secretary, to organizer and colonel of the First U.S. Volunteer Calvary Regiment in the Spanish-American War (renowned as the "Rough Riders"), to the governorship of New York, to the vice presidency, and then to the presidency in 1901, following the assassination of William McKinley. In 1904, Roosevelt was elected for another term.

The drawing room, Mrs. Roosevelt's favorite room, is furnished with splendid Victorian pieces. Here, and almost everywhere else in the house, there are shelves to hold Roosevelt's large book collection.

When family members took ill, they were cared for in the second-floor sick room.

(Opposite) In 1884, Theodore Roosevelt contracted a Long Island architectural firm to build this large Victorian home on his wooded Oyster Bay property. He called the estate "Sagamore Hill," after an Indian chief who once ruled the area.

(Previous pages) This close-up shows the gears of the 19th-century yarn winder in the Long Island home of Walt Whitman. (see pp. 48-50)

The North Room—built in 1905 with mahogany, black walnut, swamp cypress, and hazel—houses Roosevelt's books, flags, and hunting trophies.

During his years in political office, Roosevelt often returned to Sagamore Hill with his wife and six children. As President, he entertained heads of state there. In 1905, he achieved a cease-fire (and later peace treaty) between warring Japan and Russia by mediating an agreement between their ambassadors (reportedly in his library). For this achievement, he was awarded the Nobel Peace Prize in 1906.

After his White House years, Roosevelt retired to Sagamore Hill, though he did make one more run for the presidency in 1912 with the short-lived Progressive ("Bull Moose")

Party. After that defeat, he left his home only for lecture tours and for big-game hunting junkets around the world. He died in his sleep at Sagamore Hill on January 6, 1919, and was buried at Young's Cemetery not far from his home. Edith Roosevelt lived at Sagamore Hill until her death in 1948. Two years later the estate was acquired by the Theodore Roosevelt Association. In 1963, it was donated to the American people and is today administered by the National Park Service. Visitors can view Roosevelt's home, his gravesite, and Old Orchard Museum, once the home of Theodore Roosevelt, Jr.

The top floor of the house is devoted to Roosevelt's extensive gun collection. He sometimes used the room for writing when family activities prevented him from working in the ground-floor library.

Roosevelt's ornately hand-carved bed won a prize at the 1876 Philadelphia Exposition.

Today, the area surrounding Walt Whitman's birthplace on Old Walt Whitman Road in Huntington Station, New York, is crowded and bustling. Just to the north lies the heavily traveled Jericho Turnpike, and beyond that, the Long Island Railroad. Not far behind the house, across busy Route 110, lies the Walt Whitman Mall, crowded with shoppers. But in 1819, when the great poet was born, thick woods and wide fields dominated the area; only an occasional farmhouse suggested that settlers had indeed arrived.

The house of Whitman's birth was built between 1810 and 1819 by his father, Walter, for his wife, Louisa, and their growing family —the poet had eight siblings. The 2½-story farmhouse was constructed of hand-hewn beams, held together by wooden pegs, and set on a foundation of small boulders. A corbeled chimney rises from one end of the house, and large pane windows admit light and air. It is

believed that a small wing to the right of the front door as one faces it is older than the rest of the house.

In Whitman's time, the interior was probably arranged to suit the needs of a typical farm family—with kitchen, parlor, and dining room on the main floor and bedrooms upstairs. Also on the first floor, next to the parlor, was the "borning room," a feature not unusual in houses occupied by large farm families, where the poet might well have been born. Surrounding the home were the fields and orchards worked by the Whitmans.

The family lived in the house until 1823. When young Walt was four years old, his father, a better carpenter than farmer, moved the family to Brooklyn, New York, to take advantage of a projected housing boom. Walt lived in Brooklyn for about 15 years but made frequent trips to Long Island relatives.

Whitman's parents were barely literate, but young Walt took an interest in reading. As

Walt Whitman, one of America's greatest poets, was born in this Long island farmhouse, built by his father, in 1819.

(Opposite) The Whitmans' kitchen with its bare wooden floors is simply furnished, as it would have been during the early 19th century.

a teenager, he apprenticed himself to a Brooklyn printer. He later worked as a compositor for two Long Island newspapers. At age 19, he moved back to the Huntington area and founded, edited, and managed his own weekly newspaper, the *Long Islander.* A year later, after that enterprise had failed, he returned to the city, where he continued his career as a newspaper editor, using his spare time to travel and write poetry. In 1855, he published the first edition of *Leaves of Grass,* a collection of rambling free-verse poems that established him as a poet with a uniquely American voice.

Although Whitman lived on the Huntington farm for only a few years and traveled extensively, the house and the landscape made a lasting impression on him. In "A Song of Joys," he celebrated his boyhood years, saying, "O to go back to the place where I was born, / To hear the birds sing once more, / To ramble about the house and barn and over the fields once more, / And through the orchard and along the old lanes once more." In "Out of the Cradle Endlessly Rocking," he reminisced about the "patches of briers and blackberries," the "musical shuttle" of "the mocking-bird's throat," and other sights and sounds of his Long Island youth. His ability to unite the disparate experiences of his childhood and adulthood years into a single poetic vision—a celebration of the American landscape and character—earned him the title "bard of democracy." He continued writing poetry until his death in 1892.

The farm which the Whitmans sold in 1823 had only three more owners until 1949. Then the house was acquired by the newly formed Walt Whitman Birthplace Association to prevent it from becoming a roadhouse tavern. The association continues to maintain the house in cooperation with the New York State Office of Parks, Recreation, and Historic Preservation.

Today, the main floor of the home is restored to its condition in Whitman's time. The upper floor, its fireplace still intact, now holds the Walt Whitman Library, which is used by poets and Whitman scholars from all over the country. The exhibit room next to the library displays pictures of the poet.

This early 19th-century yarn winder, a staple in turn-of-the-century farmhouses, is set in the second-floor exhibit room.

The poet might well have been born in this room, located on the first floor of the house.

The diminutive lady was a real patriot and a congenital rebel. She took the sacrifice of two husbands to the Cause in her stride and worked tirelessly to produce the large quantity of new flags that her first sample had generated.

Aldred W. Scott
Betsy Ross's great-great-great grandson

An unknown artist's impression of Betsy Ross. (Ms. Ross, being a Quaker, would have been unlikely to sit for a portrait; few, if any, generally accepted portraits of her exist)

THE BETSY ROSS HOUSE at 239 Arch Street in the Old City section of Philadelphia is significant for two reasons: first, it is a fine example of mid-18th-century artisan-class urban architecture; and, second, it was the home and workplace of Betsy Ross, the patriot and seamstress who sewed the first American flag.

Elizabeth Griscom was born on January 1, 1752, the seventh daughter of the 17 children born to Samuel and Rebecca James Griscom. In November 1773, she eloped with John Ross, and the young couple rented a 2½-story red-brick Georgian-style house, built around 1740, to serve as a home and a workplace for their upholstery business. Their clients would include Benjamin Franklin, the Society of Free Quakers, and the State House of Pennsylvania.

Betsy and John set up the front parlor of their Arch Street house as a showroom for their goods and used the rear parlor, behind the stairway, as their living room. The kitchen was in the basement. The second-floor front

This artisan-class brick house on Arch Street in Philadelphia was both a home and place of business for Betsy Ross.

bedroom was occupied by John and Betsy, and the rear bedroom was later used by her children from her second and third marriages. The small rooms on the top floor were for guests or apprentice workers.

Like many other young Philadelphians, John and Betsy were involved in the patriot cause. Following the outbreak of the Revolutionary War, Betsy made flags for the Pennsylvania Navy and musket balls for the Continental army. John joined the army and was killed in one of the early skirmishes in January 1776, leaving Betsy a widow at age 24.

During the spring after her husband's death, Betsy's uncle by marriage, George Ross, a friend of Gen. George Washington and a signer of the Declaration of Independence, paid a visit to the house on Arch Street. With him were Robert Morris, another leader in the patriot cause, and General Washington himself. Their purpose was to ask Betsy to make a flag for the Continental army. Until then, the Continentals had used a flag bearing, in part, the Union Jack, combined with seven red stripes alternating with six white stripes. Washington thought the Union Jack inappropriate for an army fighting the British crown. He had in mind keeping the red and white stripes but replacing the Union Jack with a blue field having 13 white stars. Betsy contributed two important features: she recommended five-point stars rather than those with six points, and she suggested that the stars be arranged in a circle, the symbol of unity. Washington liked her ideas, and in the rear parlor of her home the visitors agreed to have Betsy Ross sew the first American flag.

A year later Betsy married Joseph Ashburn, and the couple had two children. Ash-

An 18th-century pencil-post bed, reached by a two-step riser, dominates Betsy Ross's second-floor bedroom. The window is covered by venetian blinds with wooden slats, introduced to America around 1750.

This kitchen table holds a spice chest and other utensils from the mid-18th century.

The fireplace in the rear parlor is bordered by tile imported from the Netherlands. An unfinished American flag like the one Betsy Ross created in this house lies on a worktable.

burn, a sea captain, was captured by the British and died in an English prison in 1782. She married John Claypoole in 1783, and three years later, after their second child was born, the family moved to larger quarters on Second Street near the docks. The couple had three more children, and Betsy worked as a seamstress for another 40 years. She died on January 30, 1836, at age 84, at her daughter's home in Abington, Pennsylvania, outside of Philadelphia.

Following Betsy's departure from Arch Street, the house was occupied by various artisans and tenants who modified it somewhat over the years. In 1935, A. Atwater Kent, a pioneer in the radio business, bought the house and began to restore it to its 18th-century appearance. On June 14, 1937—Flag Day—he gave the home to the city of Philadelphia, which continues to maintain it. Visitors to the Betsy Ross House can visit other historical sites in downtown Philadelphia, such as Independence Hall and Carpenters' Hall, which Betsy's father helped build, both part of Independence National Historical Park.

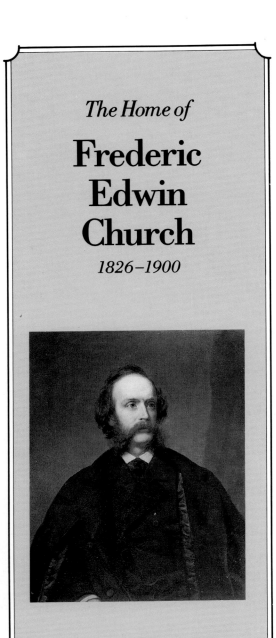

I am appalled when I look at the magnificent scenery which encircles my clumsy studio, and then glance at the painted oilcloth on my easel.

Painting attributed to Charles Loring Elliott. 1866. New York State Office of Parks, Recreation and Historic Preservation. Bureau of Historic Sites. Olana State Historic Site, Taconic Region.

The studio, built in the late 1880s, is designed for a left-handed artist; rheumatism forced Church to become a southpaw late in life.

OLANA, THE ESTATE of Frederic Church, combines the landscape artist's two great affections: breathtaking natural vistas and Middle Eastern architecture. The home, located on a high summit south of Hudson, New York, resembles a Persian palace, overlooking a deep valley between the high wooded banks of the Hudson River.

By the 1860s, Church was the preeminent landscape painter in the United States and a leading member of the second generation of Hudson River school artists. His immense painting *Niagara*, completed in 1857, made him not only the best known but also the best paid painter in the country. Anxious to build a home suitable for his family, Church began buying parcels of land in Hudson along the banks of the river for which the town was named. He knew the area well. In the 1840s, the English-born artist Thomas Cole had owned land directly across the river from Church's new property. Cole had been one of his teachers; in fact, one of young Frederic's sketches, dated 1845, portrayed the view from the property that he was to own 20 years later.

In 1867, after Church bought the final piece of land for his estate—the summit on which the house now sits—he began to plan his home. First, he enlisted Richard Morris Hunt, the architect who would later become famous for Beaux Arts villas like Biltmore and The Breakers (see pp. 108–111 and 32–35, respectively). But shortly afterward, Church embarked on a long tour of the Middle East and became fascinated with Persian architecture. On his return to America, he scrapped Hunt's plans and hired Calvert Vaux. Church himself did most of the sketches for the house, and he relied on Vaux to turn the plans into a building.

The work began in 1870. Church and his family took up residence in 1872 when the second floor was ready for occupancy, but construction and interior decoration continued until 1874. The result of six years of work was a huge palace with quarry-faced ashlar walls, a massive tower with balconies overlooking the river valley, and pointed Islamic arched door and window frames. Church called his home "Olana," after a

Frederic Church's Persian palace sits atop
a high hill overlooking the Hudson River.

palace in ancient Persia. (*Olana* is close to the
Arabic word *Alana*, meaning "our place on
high.")

Inside, the Court Hall, shaped like a
Greek cross, serves as a greeting area and
junction for the other first-floor rooms—the
library, dining room, sitting room, and parlor.
Doors to these rooms are stenciled in silver
and gold; the walls are decorated with Church's
paintings and the works of other artists whom
Church admired. A two-tiered stairway leads
to two large second-floor bedrooms. An imposing tinted window atop the first flight of
stairs casts amber light on the room below.

Olana was magnificent, but Church, never
quite satisfied with the result, continued to
devise modifications. In the 1880s, when he
was no longer publicly exhibiting his paintings,

he designed a new studio wing. Connected to
the main house by two rooms and a colon-
nade, the addition is Mexican in style, not Persian, the artist having been influenced by several south-of-the-border vacations. Interestingly, the studio is arranged for a left-handed
artist; by the 1880s, Church could hardly paint
right-handed because of arthritis.

Church lived at Olana until his death in
1900. The home then passed to his son, Louis,
and daughter-in-law, Sally. Louis died in 1943,
but his wife lived until age 96 and kept the
house as it had been in Frederic Church's time.
When she died in 1964, the estate was purchased by the State of New York. Today Olana
is administered by the New York State Office
of Parks, Recreation, and Historic Preservation, with support from Friends of Olana, Inc.

The doorway leading to Church's studio is
flanked with portraits of the painter (right)
and his father.

The doors of Church's library are stenciled in silver and gold.

The east parlor served as a formal reception room.

I knew very little about my own people and very much about the Chinese. If I had a professional motive as a writer, it was to help my people understand the Chinese whom I knew so well.

From *China Past and Present*

Photograph. c. 1938. Library of Congress.

PEARL S. BUCK was born in her family's home in Hillsboro, West Virginia, on June 26, 1892, but she spent the majority of her childhood and adult years in China, where her parents (and later she and her first husband, John L. Buck) were missionaries. Nevertheless, in 1935, when the universally acclaimed author of *The Good Earth* (1931) and many other works, was looking for a permanent home, she chose a 100-year-old stone farmhouse solidly built on the good earth of Bucks County, Pennsylvania.

The old farmhouse that Pearl Buck and her second husband, Richard J. Walsh, bought had not been occupied for 17 years and was in great need of renovation. The work began as soon as they moved in. A wing was added to the right side of the house for a new kitchen and mudroom. The old kitchen was made into an elegant dining room, and the entire first floor was enlarged. On the left side of the house, another addition was built. It included a library and reading room to hold Buck and Walsh's extensive collection of books. Today, her large Chinese Windsor desk sits in the center of the main library. Upstairs, a wall connecting two bedrooms was removed to create one large master bedroom with two fireplaces.

Perhaps Buck's most interesting renovation involved a 200-year-old stone building that stands behind the farmhouse. It was joined to the main house by an enclosed breezeway with red tile floor. Inside the old building, offices for Buck, Walsh, and secretaries were built, and a Chinese-style courtyard was placed next to the breezeway. When renovation was complete, Buck had a home perfectly suited to her needs: a 19th-century American farmhouse with Chinese accents.

Though she devoted much of her energy to her home, as always Buck still found time to write. She published *This Proud Heart* in 1937 and wrote *The Time Is Noon* shortly thereafter (though it was not published until 1967). In 1938, she received both the Nobel Prize for Literature and the Pulitzer Prize for the body of her work, the only American woman to be so honored.

Buck continued to write more than a book a year until her death in 1973, just before her 81st birthday. She was buried on the grounds of her estate, which is now maintained by the Pearl S. Buck Foundation. The foundation offers tours of the house and uses the estate as its headquarters for helping needy Amerasian children in Asia.

In 1935, Pearl S. Buck and her husband purchased this century-old farmhouse, solidly built on the good earth of Bucks County, Pennsylvania.

In 1887, Thomas Edison purchased this impressive 23-room Victorian mansion, Glenmont, in the exclusive Llewellyn Park section of West Orange, New Jersey.

THOMAS EDISON was born in 1847 in a two-story brick home, now restored as the Birthplace of Thomas Alva Edison, in Milan, Ohio. As a young man, he worked as a telegrapher and tinkered with machines. His hobby cost him a job early in his career, but it also led to his first patent in 1869, for a vote recorder, the ancestor of today's mechanical ballot boxes. A year later, he invented a new ticker tape machine to record stock market activity and sold it for a large profit, which he used to set up his own shop in Newark, New Jersey. During the next 17 years, he developed many of the inventions that led to his 1093 lifetime patents. In 1887, after working in Menlo Park, New Jersey, and New York City (as well as Newark), he decided to build a bigger lab in West Orange, New Jersey.

A year earlier, Edison, a widower, had remarried. As a wedding present to his new wife, Mina, he purchased a large Victorian home in the impressive Llewellyn Park section of West Orange. The mansion, called

"Glenmont," had been built six years earlier by Henry C. Pedder, a New York executive.

The 23-room brick and wood mansion stands 3½ stories tall with handsome gables and balconies. Large chimneys poke through the roof, and a rooftop balustrade provides a splendid view of the surrounding woods. In constructing Glenmont, Pedder had used only the best materials, including bluestone block from Connecticut and expensive pressed bricks from Baltimore. It was a fitting home for the world-famous Edison and his new wife.

The interior of the house is equally impressive. The ground floor holds a large reception room with a noble fireplace, a formal drawing room that leads to a conservatory filled with plants, a kitchen, and a large dining room. A grand mahogany staircase off the reception room leads to the second floor, which holds the family sitting room. This room also served as Edison's library and is equipped with desks for both Thomas and Mina.

Edison spent most of his time on the second floor. He claimed that the sitting room, with its large picture window and the bedroom, with its glass doors leading to a balcony, inspired his best inventions. He referred to his desk in that room as his "thought bench."

The top floors of the mansion contain bedrooms for Thomas and Mina, for their six children (three from his first marriage), and for their many guests. Visitors to the estate included Woodrow Wilson, Herbert Hoover, Charles A. Lindbergh, Helen Keller, George Eastman, and Edison's neighbor from Milan, Ohio, Henry Ford.

About a mile from Glenmont, Edison set up his West Orange laboratory. The main building is three stories high and 250 feet long, housing machine shops, an engine room, photography rooms, glass blowing rooms, and a library with more than 10,000 volumes. While at West Orange, Edison invented some of his most ingenious devices, including the prototypes of today's phonograph and the motion picture projector. After working at the lab — he often stayed there for days at a stretch — he returned to the luxury of his nearby home.

Thomas Edison died in an upstairs bedroom at Glenmont in 1931, at age 84. Mina lived until 1947. The Edisons are buried side by side in simple plots behind the home in which they lived together for 45 years.

Since 1954, the National Park Service has maintained Glenmont and Edison's nearby laboratory. Before touring the home, visitors can travel one mile east to the lab on Main Street and Lakeside Avenue. Of special interest there is an exact reproduction of the "Black Maria," the world's first motion picture theater.

Edison built his laboratory about a mile from Glenmont; the chemical lab is shown here.

60

Thomas Edison was born in this simple brick house in Milan, Ohio.

(Opposite) Glenmont's tastefully furnished second-floor library has three levels of bookshelves.

The Edisons vacationed at this large home in Ft. Myers, Florida.

To all general purposes we have uniformly been one people; each individual citizen everywhere enjoying the same national rights, privileges, and protection.

From *The Federalist Papers*

Engraving by Asher B. Durand from a painting by Gilbert Stuart. c. 1783. Library of Congress.

L IKE THE ADAMS family estate in Braintree, Massachusetts (see pp. 18–19), the Jay homestead in Katonah, New York, remained the residence of a single family for several generations. From 1790 to 1953, five generations of Jays lived in the rambling 2½-story house on land originally acquired by John Jay's grandfather, Jacobus Van Cortlandt, from Katonah, an Indian chief, in 1703.

The first Jay to live in Katonah was the builder of the family home, John Jay—Chief Justice of New York State, President of the Second Continental Congress, key negotiator of the Treaty of Paris (1783) and the later Jay Treaty (1794) with Great Britain, coauthor of *The Federalist* papers, first Chief Justice of the U.S. Supreme Court, and Governor of New York. In 1787, two years before he accepted President George Washington's invitation to serve as Chief Justice, Jay designed and commissioned a modest home to be built on the property that he inherited in Katonah. While the structure was primarily intended for the estate manager, Jay made use of it himself when circuit riding in the area as part of his judicial duties. In 1797, after the birth of a fifth child, Jay looked ahead to his retirement from public life and asked his eldest son, Peter Augustus, to make the Katonah property

suitable for the family's future home. After creating a second structure for the farm manager, Peter expanded the 6-room cottage into a 24-room Federal style home. He replaced the gabled roof with a gambrel roof, added a wing to each side of the house to accommodate a new kitchen and an office, and turned the front porch into a veranda running the length of the house.

When Jay completed his second term as Governor of New York and returned to Katonah in 1801, his home was ready. It had a large formal parlor and dining room, pleasant kitchen facilities, a comfortable office where Jay could conduct his correspondence, a wine cellar, and a sufficient number of upstairs bedrooms to accommodate the family. In 1818, however, after Jay's third grandchild was born—the son of William and Augusta Jay—another wing was added to the house to meet the needs of the growing family and its frequent guests.

Jay lived comfortably in the family home until his death in 1829. His youngest son, William, a judge and active abolitionist, inherited the estate and lived there with his six children. When he died in 1858, he bequeathed the home to his son, John Jay II, also

This desk was specially built for John Jay in the late 1780s.

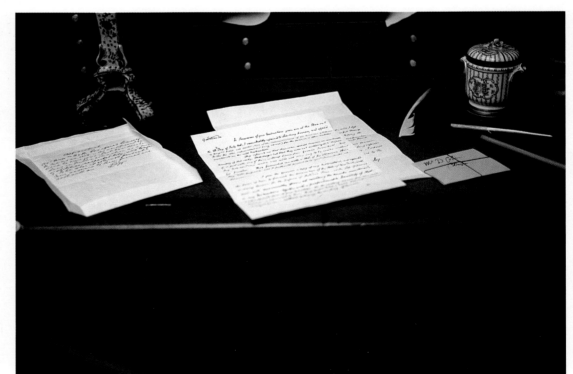

Five generations of Jays lived in this splendid colonial home in Katonah, New York.

a fierce abolitionist and, later, a diplomat in the administration of Ulysses S. Grant. John II, at his wife's suggestion, modernized the interior and exterior to give the house a Victorian look.

Just as each generation of Adamses remodeled Peacefield to suit its needs, each owner of the Katonah estate reworked the Federal home that John Jay built. In 1904, John Jay II's son, William II, extended the north wing. The next owner, Eleanor Jay Iselin, who inherited the estate in 1915, added a large west wing featuring a handsome wood-paneled

ballroom with portraits of John Jay and others of his family, as well as George Washington, Thomas Jefferson, and John Adams.

In 1954 the County of Westchester purchased the homestead and adjoining acreage; subsequently, it was turned over to New York State. Aspects of the house have been recreated to reflect John Jay's occupancy during the first quarter of the 19th century. Other rooms, and portions of the exterior, as well as the grounds and outbuildings, reflect the tastes of the five generations of Jays who lived there during the home's 200-year history.

The formal parlor in the Anthonys' home is furnished with handsome Victorian pieces. Susan's portrait hangs above the fireplace.

THE UNOFFICIAL headquarters of the women's rights movement of the late-19th and early-20th centuries was a handsome red-brick house with a shingled Queen Anne front gable on 17 Madison Street in Rochester, New York. The home belonged to Lucy Anthony and her two daughters, Mary and Susan.

Susan Brownell Anthony was born in Adams, Massachusetts, in 1820 to Quaker parents. When she was a child, the family moved to western New York, where she received her education and began her teaching career. As a young woman, she continued the family's activist tradition by joining the temperance movement. Finding that, as a woman, she was not allowed to speak at temperance rallies, she decided to devote her energy to the movement to win women the right to vote ("woman suffrage"), and shortly thereafter became an active participant in the cause.

In 1866, Susan, her mother, and her sister moved to Rochester and bought the Victorian home on Madison Street. The dwelling, built in 1859, consists of two full stories and two attic rooms and has front and rear porches. The front yard is small, but the back yard was large enough to accommodate a sizable garden and a barn during the Anthonys' time.

The first floor contains an entrance hallway and four main rooms—a formal parlor with a fireplace at the front of the house, a sitting room with a small adjoining sewing or study alcove, a large dining room, and a kitchen leading to the rear porch. A handsome mahogany staircase, flanked by a wall with stained-glass windows, leads to the second-floor bedrooms.

The room at the front of the house, above the parlor, was Mrs. Anthony's sleeping quarters; today, it is a museum room containing mementos of the woman-suffrage movement, including the desk at which Carrie Chapman Catt drafted the 19th Amendment. The second floor also includes four other bedrooms — used by Susan, Mary, and guests — as well as Susan's study. The third-floor rooms were used as workrooms. In one, Susan helped write the monumental *History of Woman Suffrage.*

During the 42 years that Susan B. Anthony lived on Madison Street, the house was bustling with activity. Stanton, Frederick Douglass, and other civil libertarians, were frequent visitors, organizing their efforts, planning their demonstrations, and writing their manifestos. The movement's early days were marked by both victories and setbacks. In 1869, the National Woman Suffrage Association, with Anthony spearheading the attack, campaigned for a constitutional amendment guaranteeing women the right to vote. That measure, presented to 40 consecutive sessions of Congress, continually failed to pass. An attempt to have women included in the 14th Amendment, which secured voting rights for all adult males, also failed. In 1872, Anthony was arrested in the family parlor for attempting to vote in the presidential election. She was tried and fined for violating the state's voting laws, but she refused to pay. In 1898, however, Anthony was successful in convincing the University of Rochester to admit female students.

The 19th Amendment, giving voting rights to all women, did not pass until 1920, 14 years after Anthony's death. Nonetheless, it is often called the "Anthony Amendment" as a tribute to the woman who worked so hard to have it accepted.

In 1907, after Mary Anthony died, the family's home was sold. Only two owners had possession of it between 1907 and 1945, when Mrs. George Howard, president of the Rochester Federation of Women's Clubs, an organization founded in 1889, purchased the house to preserve it as a memorial to one of the city's most famous citizens. Today, the building is owned and maintained by the Susan B. Anthony Memorial, Inc.

In 1864, Susan B. Anthony, her sister, and their mother moved into this five-year-old Victorian home on Madison Street in Rochester, New York, where the suffragette lived for 42 years.

The Home of
Washington Irving
1783–1859

I am always at a loss to know how much to believe of my own stories.

From *Tales of a Traveler*

Engraving from a painting by John Wesley Jarvis. 1809. Library of Congress.

WASHINGTON IRVING, born in New York City in 1783, was named after the great general who had just won the war against Great Britain. He spent much of the first 50 years of his life traveling abroad, first as manager of the Liverpool branch of his father's hardware business and later as a U.S. diplomat. During breaks in his career, he turned to his first love, writing, and he eventually became America's best-known author. In 1832, he returned to America after a 17-year absence, intending to retire in high style. Three years later, he bought a small cottage on the Hudson River in Tarrytown, New York, and called it "Sunnyside."

The estate and its new owner were a perfect match. Irving had a keen interest in the 17th-century Dutch settlers who lived along the Hudson. His most popular book, *The Sketch Book of Geoffrey Crayon, Gent.*, published in 1820, contained several tales of the New York Dutch, including two, "The Legend of Sleepy Hollow" and "Rip Van Winkle," which were destined to become American classics. Indeed, his small late-17th-century Tarrytown cottage had once belonged to the Van Tassel family, the name he used in the tale of the headless horseman. Right after the purchase, Irving, with the assistance of George Harvey, a well-known architect, directed extensive remodeling to enlarge the cottage, employing the various architectural styles that he had grown fond of overseas, such as stepped Dutch gables and Gothic windows. He also added weathervanes from old New York buildings and, about 10 years later, built an extension with a pagoda-shaped roof to house extra guest rooms. The grounds surrounding this pleasant cottage include a large number of trees, a stream, a pond, and a waterfall.

The first floor comprises a parlor with a rosewood piano, a dining room overlooking the Hudson River, and a "modern" kitchen

Washington Irving's cottage in Tarrytown, New York, features stepped Dutch gables, Gothic windows, and weathervanes from old New York buildings.

with a wood-burning cooking stove and a hot water heater. Across the hall from the dining room is Irving's study, which features a large fireplace and wood bookcases trimmed with a brilliant scarlet curtain. In the center of the room sits the author's writing desk, a gift from his publisher. Also on the first floor is a small picture gallery which contains some of Irving's drawings. The second floor holds several arched bedrooms. All of the interiors reflect Irving's diversified taste, with decorative items brought back from his many overseas trips. No wonder he wrote that he would not trade Sunnyside "for any chateau in Christendom!"

A few years after moving to Sunnyside, Irving was nominated for Mayor of New York; he later received an offer from President Martin Van Buren to serve as Secretary of the Navy. But he preferred life at Sunnyside to the political battles of New York and Washington. However, he did leave his home from 1842 to 1846 to serve as U.S. Minister to Spain.

The author continued to write in his later years. While living at Sunnyside, he oversaw G. P. Putnam's revised edition of his entire canon, 15 volumes in all. He also wrote a five-volume *Life of George Washington*. Irving died on November 28, 1859, at age 76, in his upstairs bedroom. He is buried in nearby Sleepy Hollow Cemetery in Tarrytown.

After Irving's death, Sunnyside came into the possession of the author's brother Ebenezer and his two nieces, who had lived at Sunnyside for many years. Members of the Irving family owned the property until 1945, when it was purchased by John D. Rockefeller, Jr. Restoration began shortly thereafter. A large wing, added around the turn of the century, was removed, and the interior was restored to its condition in Irving's day. The final restoration of the 1847 tower and kitchen yard was completed in 1961, by Sleepy Hollow Restorations (now Historic Hudson Valley), which administers three other Hudson River estates and the Union Church of Pocantico Hills.

Irving's nieces played the rosewood piano in the parlor; the author accompanied them on the flute.

Irving's study contains the author's sturdy writing desk, a gift from his publisher.

The tale proper, in our opinion, affords unquestionably the fairest field for the exercise of the loftiest talent, which can be afforded by the wide domains of mere prose.

From his reviews of Nathaniel Hawthorne's *Twice Told Tales*

Photograph. c. 1848. Library of Congress.

EDGAR ALLAN POE, considered by some to be the father of the American short story, and also an important poet and literary critic, never lived in one place very long. He was born in Boston in 1809, the child of traveling actors, but his father left the family shortly after his birth and his mother died when he was two years old. He was taken to the Richmond, Virginia, home of John and Frances Allan, who fostered but never legally adopted him. For a time, the Allans moved the family to England, and Poe lived in boarding schools. When the family returned home, Poe attended the University of Virginia. In 1827, he moved to Boston after a quarrel with his foster father. Poe later served in the U.S. Army and, in 1830/31, attended West Point but was dismissed for breaking rules. Then he began an 18-year career as a writer and editor that took him to New York, Philadelphia, and Baltimore. He never owned a home.

After Poe's year in West Point, he moved in with his grandmother Elizabeth Poe and his aunt Maria Clemm on Wilks Street in Baltimore. In the fall of 1832, Poe, his grandmother, his aunt, and her daughter, Virginia, later Poe's wife, moved to a 2½-story brick home on North Amity Street at the western edge of town. Their new abode, built around 1830, contained a parlor and kitchen on the first floor, two second-floor bedrooms—one for Mrs. Poe, and one for Mrs. Clemm and Virginia—and an attic room for Poe; his study was housed in a small gable at the front of the house.

During the three years that Poe lived on North Amity Street, he published several short stories, including "MS. Found in a Bottle," which won a $50 prize in a contest sponsored by the *Saturday Visitor* of Baltimore. He looked for a full-time newspaper job, but didn't find one. In 1835, the Clemms and Poe moved to Richmond.

During the next 15 years, Poe edited several publications and wrote many of the stories and poems that later made him famous, among which were such tales of suspense as "Murders in the Rue Morgue," "The Tell-Tale Heart," and "The Purloined Letter," as well as such melodious though dark poems as "Annabelle Lee" and "The Raven." His literary successes, however, did not bring great financial rewards or even a steady income. Thus, he blamed himself when, in 1847, his 25-year-old wife died of consumption. Two years later, he collapsed on a Baltimore street during a business trip and died a few days later.

The North Amity Street house had more than 20 tenants in the years after Poe's departure. It was vacant from the mid-1920s until 1949, when it was turned into the privately owned Edgar Allan Poe House and Museum. In 1979, it was acquired by the City of Baltimore. Other sites honoring the great writer include the Poe Museum in Richmond, the Edgar Allan Poe National Historic Site in Philadelphia, and Edgar Allan Poe Cottage, his last home, in the Bronx, New York.

Edgar Allan Poe lived in this brick house on North Amity Street in Baltimore with his grandmother, aunt, and cousin for three years.

The grandsons of Commodore Cornelius Vanderbilt, the shipping and railroad magnate of the mid-19th century, are responsible for some of America's most impressive homes, including The Breakers (see pp. 32–35) and Marble House in Newport, Rhode Island, and Biltmore in Asheville, North Carolina (see pp. 108–111). Somewhat more modest in size—yet still impressive—is Frederick Vanderbilt's mansion on the east bank of the Hudson River in Hyde Park, New York.

In 1895, when he was not quite 40 years old, Frederick Vanderbilt bought the 700-acre estate on which his mansion now stands from Walter Langdon, Jr. It was to serve as a spring and autumn home for himself and his wife, Louise, and as a farm for his purebred livestock. Vanderbilt intended to renovate the Langdon mansion, but when his architects—McKim, Mead, & White of New York City—judged the 50-year-old home to be structurally unsafe, he commissioned the firm to design a new house in the Beaux Arts style of the day. A temporary residence (now the Visitors' Center) was built for the Vanderbilts, Langdon's home was razed (though some of the outbuildings were left standing), and in 1896 construction began on a new home on a bluff overlooking the Hudson River.

The new three-story 54-room mansion, which cost the Vanderbilts $660,000, was completed late in 1898. Like The Breakers, it is faced with Indiana limestone. A semicircular porch in back of the house provides a splendid view of the river and beyond.

Inside, the front door opens to the magnificent main hall, where guests were greeted during formal receptions. To the left, occupying an entire wing of the house, is the 30-by-50-foot drawing room. The opposite wing houses a formal dining room of equal size. The first floor also contains a den, a study (where Vanderbilt conducted his business affairs), and several service rooms. The house is ornately decorated with furnishings from France as well as a few pieces from Italy.

The second floor houses the Vanderbilts' bedrooms and several guest rooms. Louise Vanderbilt's room is decorated in the style of

In 1898, this 54-room mansion was completed on Frederick Vanderbilt's 700-acre estate in Hyde Park, New York, a short carriage ride away from the Roosevelt estate.

The living room, used for formal
entertaining and for musical recitals,
features a marble fireplace, Florentine
tapestries, and Chinese lamps.

Louis XV, and its custom-made rug weighs more than a ton. Next door is Frederick's room, with its carved walnut woodwork and 17th-century Flemish tapestries. The top floor contains servants' quarters.

When the Vanderbilts lived at Hyde Park, they were in good company. Not far away was the Roosevelt mansion, and upriver were the Astor and Livingston estates. They played host to captains of industry, and European nobility, including the 9th Duke of Marlborough, who married one of the Vanderbilts' nieces, Consuelo.

Frederick Vanderbilt, however, was a private person who preferred the life of a country gentleman to that of a gracious host. He saw his estate as the just reward of a successful businessman who needed an occasional respite from his duties in New York City. Accordingly, he took great delight in managing estate affairs. In 1901 he supervised the construction of new barns to house his prize herds, and two years later he helped design new gardens.

He took a lively interest in horticulture, entering his Hyde Park plants and flowers in the Dutchess County Horticultural Society shows and county fairs. He also enjoyed trips on his oceangoing yacht.

Frederick Vanderbilt became a widower in 1926, and he died at Hyde Park 12 years later, at age 82. The Vanderbilts were childless, and after their deaths the estate passed to Margaret Van Alen, a niece on Mrs. Vanderbilt's side and a frequent Hyde Park visitor. Unable to sell the estate at acceptable terms, Margaret chose to donate the home and 212 surrounding acres to the federal government. The estate was named a National Historic Site in December 1940 and is now administered by the National Park Service.

This winding stairway leads to the family bedrooms on the second floor.

The headboard and dressers in Frederick Vanderbilt's bedroom, designed to match the woodwork, are made of carved Circassian walnut.

The formal dining room features scarlet-covered court chairs and a table that could be expanded to seat 30 guests.

Clara Barton

1821–1912

CLARA BARTON'S life was inseparable from her work—administering to the wounded on the battlefield, providing relief for victims of natural disasters, and offering shelter to the homeless. Not surprisingly, her house in Glen Echo, Maryland, was both her home and a headquarters of the American Red Cross, which she founded.

Barton was born in a small clapboard farmhouse in North Oxford, Massachusetts, in 1821. Teaching was her first career, but when her voice began to fail she moved to Washington, D.C., to work as a copyist. When the Civil War began, she started gathering supplies for the Union army. Her reputation for kindness and hard work spread, and in 1864 she was appointed superintendent of nurses for the Army of the James. Near the end of the conflict, she began an effort—with President Lincoln's support—to find missing soldiers.

After the war, she traveled to Switzerland for a vacation and to ease her bronchitis. There she met representatives of the International Red Cross, who urged her to establish an American branch of the growing organization. When she returned to the United States, she did so, founding the first American chapter in Dansville, New York, in 1881. In the years to follow, she and the organization assisted thousands of victims of natural disasters and epidemics. After the Johnstown flood of 1889,

for example, she had Red Cross hotels built in the Pennsylvania city to shelter the area's homeless. She also brought relief to the wounded in the Spanish-American War.

In 1891 she erected a large building on land given her by two real estate developers in Glen Echo, Maryland, several miles from Washington, D.C., to serve as a Red Cross headquarters. As it was without heat or plumbing, it was suitable only as a warehouse, so the organization's offices continued to be maintained in Washington. In 1897, however, the 75-year-old Barton renovated the Glen Echo building. Bare pine walls were covered with muslin for painting, comfortable living quarters were created, and the building was given a face-lift.

The 38-room Victorian structure became Barton's home and the official Red Cross headquarters. Parlors doubled as reception rooms, and the long halls were lined with supply closets. Moreover, Barton turned the property into a working farm with chickens, cows, and vegetable gardens.

In 1904, Clara resigned from the Red Cross. She died at her Glen Echo home in 1912, at age 90, and was buried in the family cemetery in North Oxford, Massachusetts.

Today the home of Clara Barton on 5801 Oxford Road in Glen Echo, Maryland, is a National Historic Site, administered by the National Park Service.

In this reception room, Barton met with statesmen, benefactors, and Red Cross representatives from other nations.

The hallways of the Glen Echo building are lined with closets to hold Red Cross supplies.

In Clara Barton's time, this staff office was bustling with activity.

Clara Barton's home in Glen Echo, Maryland, also served as a headquarters for the American Red Cross.

Franklin D. Roosevelt

1882–1945

I pledge you, I pledge myself, a new deal for the American people.

From his acceptance speech at the Democratic National Convention, 1932

Photograph by Leon A. Perskie. c. 1938. Franklin D. Roosevelt Library.

FRANKLIN D. ROOSEVELT, who perhaps did more for American working people than any other U.S. President, was the only child of privileged Hudson River gentry. He was born on the family estate in Hyde Park, New York, in 1882, and maintained his permanent residence there throughout his life. He was buried in the rose garden on the estate, according to his wishes, on April 15, 1945; Eleanor, his wife and partner of 40 years, is buried beside him.

In 1867, the Hyde Park property was purchased by Roosevelt's father, James, a descendent of 17th-century Dutch settlers. James Roosevelt originally bought 110 acres of land and a modest two-story structure built in about 1826. He called his new estate "Springwood," after the many natural springs in the area.

Ultimately the estate included about 900 acres, and the house was enlarged by a two-story wing at each end (which gave the home its present H-shaped configuration). In addition, a wide terrace was built in front of the house, in the style of a Georgian mansion.

Inside, the house contains 30 rooms, about a third of those for hired help and the

In 1867, James Roosevelt, the father of the future President, purchased a modest two-story home in Hyde Park, New York; in subsequent years, he added large wings to either side and a wide front terrace.

rest for the Roosevelt family. The oldest part contains the entrance hall, the dining room, and the drawing room, called the "Dresden Room" owing to the style of its chandelier, mantel clock, and candelabra. The living room occupies the entire south wing; the north wing houses the kitchen and pantry. On the second floor are several bedrooms, including the one in which Franklin was born. The servants' quarters are also on this floor. The carefully landscaped estate is dotted with trees and adorned with splendid gardens. Outbuildings include a stable that once housed the Roosevelts' prize-winning carriage horses.

James Roosevelt died while Franklin was a freshman at Harvard. Young Roosevelt later attended Columbia University Law School, was admitted to the bar in 1907, and then embarked on his remarkable political career, becoming a state senator (1911/12), then

Assistant Secretary of the Navy in the Wilson administration (1913–1920). Despite contracting polio in 1921, an illness that left him paralyzed from the waist down, he returned to politics and, in 1929, won election as Governor of New York. In 1932, he easily defeated the Republican incumbent, Herbert Hoover, to become the 32nd President of the United States.

As President, he sought to relieve the millions of Americans suffering through the Depression. His social programs, called the "New Deal," included Social Security for the aged, government support for destitute farmers, and massive construction projects for the unemployed. After the Japanese attack on Pearl Harbor, December 7, 1941, Roosevelt became a dynamic Commander in Chief, leading the nation in its drive against the Axis powers up to his untimely death in April 1945, one month before V-E (Victory in Europe) day.

Despite the demands of public office, FDR returned often to his Hyde Park home. He delivered some of his famous fireside chats there; he entertained foreign leaders there, including the British king and queen, and Prime Minister Winston Churchill; and his children were born there.

After his death, the family estate became a National Historic Site, maintained by the National Park Service. Adjacent to the home is the Roosevelt Library, which houses FDR's papers and memorabilia. It was the nation's first formal presidential library and is administered today as a branch of the National Archives.

The large living room and adjacent library fill the ground floor of the entire south wing of the house.

The South

The Home of
William Faulkner
1897–1962

I believe that man will not merely endure: he will prevail. He is immortal, not because he alone among creatures has an inexhaustible voice, but because he has a soul, a spirit capable of compassion and sacrifice and endurance. The poet's, the writer's, duty is to write about these things.

From his Nobel Prize address, 1950

Photograph. c. 1950. Library of Congress.

IN 1930, WHEN William Faulkner bought the old Colonel Sheegog place on Old Taylor Road in Oxford, Mississippi, he had already penned *Sartoris, The Sound and the Fury,* and *As I Lay Dying,* the first three novels of his Yoknapatawpha County legend, which lamented the demise of the Old South. As if he could reverse the trend that he depicted so poignantly in his fiction, he began to restore the old house to its antebellum glory.

The two-story home with the columned front portico had been built by the slaves of Col. Robert Sheegog around 1844. According to legend, Sheegog's daughter, Judith, died at the home during the Civil War when she fell from an upstairs balcony while trying to elope with a Union soldier. Neighbors maintained that her ghost wandered the grounds at night looking for her lover.

When Faulkner and his wife, Lida, moved in, the house was in shambles; but the young writer, who was also a handyman, worked tirelessly to get the place into shape. He replaced sagging beams, installed plumbing and electricity, and painted the outside. When he was finished, he had an antebellum home where he could live as a country gentleman and write his tales of the Old South. To live in high fashion, he hired a cook and manservant, even though money was tight. He named the home "Rowan Oak," after the Rowan tree, a Celtic symbol of peace and security.

The house is pleasantly situated behind a front lawn dotted with high trees. Off of the entranceway are two front parlors, one of which was used by Faulkner as a library and, before 1950, as his writing room. Family portraits by his mother hang on the walls. Opposite the library is the family parlor, where Mrs. Faulkner kept her Chickering piano. In the rear of the main floor is a hallway, used by the Faulkners as a sitting room. Here too are the dining room, kitchen, pantry, and Faulkner's later writing room/office, which he added around 1950.

The second floor contains the bedrooms. The two in front were for Jill, the Faulkners' daughter, and Victoria Franklin, Mrs. Faulkner's daughter from an earlier marriage. The middle bedroom was Faulkner's, and the one in the rear was used by his wife.

Faulkner's first ten years at Rowan Oak were the most productive of his career. From 1930 to 1940, the writer who had previously struggled to get his work published produced several of the best novels in the English language. *Sanctuary,* written in 1931, was little more than a potboiler that brought some financial security, but it was followed the next year by *Light in August.* In 1936, Faulkner

(*Previous pages*) Flowers surround Ivy Green, the antebellum Alabama farmhouse in which Helen Keller was born. (see pp. 98-101)

(*Opposite*) Faulkner's study in the rear of the house includes his writing desk and typewriter; the author spent his most productive years at Rowan Oak.

In 1930, William Faulkner purchased and restored this antebellum Mississippi house, which he named "Rowan Oak."

used the name of Robert Sheegog's daughter—Judith—to create the tragic heroine in *Absalom, Absalom!*, considered by many to be his best novel. In 1940, he published *The Hamlet* and, a year later, began work on *Go Down, Moses*, a collection of stories with "The Bear" as its centerpiece.

But Faulkner did not achieve widespread recognition or great financial rewards until the late 1940s, when Malcolm Cowley, the great literary critic, began drawing the reading public's attention to the teller of Southern tales. In 1950, after scholars had begun to review and discuss his work, Faulkner received the Nobel Prize for Literature.

Except for sojourns to the University of Virginia as a lecturer and to Hollywood as a screenwriter, Faulkner spent the last three decades of his life at Rowan Oak. He died in 1962, at age 64, and is buried in the Oxford City cemetery. Ten years later, the University of Mississippi purchased Rowan Oak from Jill Faulkner Summers to maintain it as a remembrance of Mississippi's greatest writer.

The stables behind the house held Faulkner's horses.

This informal parlor, lined with bookshelves, also served as a library. The portrait of William Faulkner above the fireplace was painted by the author's mother.

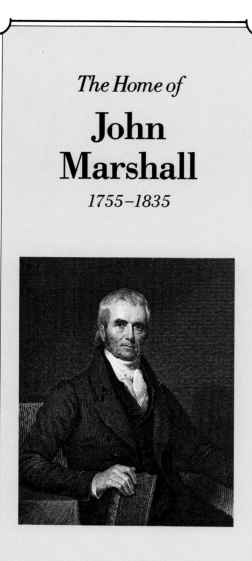
JOHN MARSHALL'S contributions to the formation of the U.S. government are often overshadowed by those of his great contemporaries — George Washington, Patrick Henry, Thomas Jefferson, and John Adams. Nonetheless, 20th-century legal scholars assert that no one did more to legitimize the new American Constitution and thereby solidify the fledgling republic than Marshall. As Justice Felix Frankfurter said a century after Marshall's tenure in office, "When Marshall came to the Supreme Court, the Constitution was essentially a virgin document. By a few opinions — a mere handful — he gave institutional direction to the inert ideas of a paper scheme of government."

Like many other great colonial statesmen, Marshall was born in Virginia and studied law as a young man. After serving with distinction during the Revolutionary War, he held a number of important judicial posts in his home state. In 1800, President John Adams named him Secretary of State, but after Marshall had served only six months in that office the President nominated him as Chief Justice of the Supreme Court. Confirmed by a unanimous vote, he remained the nation's leading judicial officer for 34 years. Perhaps his greatest decision came in the landmark case, *Marbury* v. *Madison*, in which he argued that the Supreme Court could invalidate legislation if it contradicted the principles established in or suggested by the Constitution. In effect, Marshall created the doctrine of judicial review.

Marshall's Supreme Court decisions were marked by both eloquence — a facility with language almost unmatched in the court's history — and simplicity, the ability to make complex constitutional interpretations understandable to the average citizen. Not surprisingly, his home in Richmond, Virginia, reflects these two essential qualities. Simple in outline yet dignified in appearance, the 2½-story Georgian-style brick home, now on 9th and Marshall Streets, was the Chief Justice's home from 1790, when he built it, until his death in 1835.

Marshall's estate once occupied an entire square block and included outbuildings which are no longer standing. The main house itself is fairly small. The east entry — one of three

Chief Justice John Marshall's Federal-style brick home in Richmond, Virginia, is dignified although unpretentious.

entrances, each fronted by a porch — leads to double doors and the great hall, where Marshall entertained prominent jurists and statesmen. Beyond the great hall is the dining room, with its splendid mantlepiece. To the left of the east entrance is the family parlor. A stairway in the hall leads to three second-floor bedrooms, the sleeping quarters for the Marshalls and their children.

In about 1805, Marshall also added a small wing to the northeast portion of the house, perhaps as living quarters for his maid. The home contains no special workplace for Marshall, because a law office detached from the house, and no longer standing, served that purpose. The other outbuildings included a kitchen, smokehouse, carriage house, stables, and slave quarters.

After Marshall's death in 1835, his home remained in the hands of his descendants for several decades. It was acquired by the City of Richmond in the early 1900s and turned over, in 1911, to the Association for the Preservation of Virginia Antiquities, the organization that still administers the home today.

The Home of
Booker T. Washington
1856–1915

If anywhere there are efforts to curtail the fullest growth of the Negro, let these efforts be turned into stimulating, encouraging, and making him the most useful and intelligent citizen.

From his Atlanta Exposition address

Photograph. c. 1905-10. Library of Congress.

BOOKER T. WASHINGTON'S first home was a slave cabin on the plantation of James Burroughs in Franklin County, Virginia. Plantation records show that as a youngster Booker was valued at $400. After the Civil War, an emancipated Booker and his mother moved to West Virginia, where he enrolled in elementary school and learned to read. He later attended Hampton Normal and Agricultural Institute in Virginia, where he earned his room, board, and tuition as a janitor. After graduating with honors, he began his long teaching career.

In May 1881, an unusual and challenging job opportunity came Washington's way, and he decided to take advantage of it. A group of citizens in Tuskegee, Alabama, were planning a vocational school for black youngsters and searching for a principal. They preferred a white man for the job, but when Washington's name was submitted, they offered him the position. The school, Tuskegee Institute, was officially established on July 4, 1881.

Washington kept the job for the rest of his life. The first classes were held in a dilapidated church, and the first dormitories were crude shacks, but Washington was determined to provide practical and occupational training for the children of freed slaves. He acquired land, built a campus, raised funds, and recruited an energetic faculty, including a promising young University of Iowa scientist named George Washington Carver—another ex-slave—to head Tuskegee's Department of Agriculture. Within 15 years, the school was the object of international attention. In 1905, President Theodore Roosevelt visited Tuskegee and applauded Washington's work. Grant money poured in from Andrew Carnegie, John D. Rockefeller, and others. Washington toured the country, making speeches and building good will.

During his first 18 years at Tuskegee, Washington and his family lived on campus. In 1899, however, he decided to construct a home on his own property adjacent to the school. "The Oaks," as the home came to be called, was built by students with bricks made at Tuskegee. When the students' work was completed, their principal had suitable quarters to accommodate his family and to receive important guests—a 2½-story home with Queen Anne gables and a fine wraparound porch.

The first floor of the house contains four main rooms—a family parlor, a guest bedroom, a library, and a kitchen-dining area. The din-

Booker T. Washington had humble beginnings: a slave cabin near Roanoke, Virginia.

In 1899, Washington built this brick home on his property near Tuskegee Institute.

ing facilities actually occupy two rooms—one for Washington's family and distinguished guests, the other for the home economics students who lived at The Oaks and performed household tasks as part of their schooling. The sleeping quarters are similarly divided. The second floor contains four bedrooms for the Washingtons and their three children, and the top floor has five bedrooms for students.

The second floor also includes Washington's study—furnished with pieces made at Tuskegee. Here, shortly after moving into The Oaks, he began work on his autobiography, *Up from Slavery*. The book, detailing Washington's rise from enforced servitude to international prominence, was published in 1901. Since then, it has inspired millions of students in the United States and abroad, but it has also

been the target of serious criticism. Black leaders like W.E.B. Du Bois argued that Washington overstressed occupational training for blacks at the expense of political and social advancement. But Washington believed that practical education would lead to economic independence and that political and social freedom would follow.

The Du Bois–Washington debate was unresolved when Washington died, at The Oaks, in 1915. His family occupied the home until Mrs. Washington's death in 1925. The house was then sold to Tuskegee Institute and used for administrative purposes. In 1974, Tuskegee itself was designated a National Historic Site. The National Park Service began restoring The Oaks in 1980, and the home was officially dedicated a year later.

Washington's daughter, Portia, frequently entertained the family at the piano in the living room.

Washington's study features hand-carved Oriental furniture.

The dining room at The Oaks is set for a formal dinner; evening meals were always formal affairs in the Washington home.

The Home of
Henry Morrison Flagler
1830–1913

My domain begins at Jacksonville.

Photograph by Histed Studios, Palm Beach, FL c. 1909. Henry M. Flagler Museum.

HENRY MORRISON FLAGLER, the man who "invented" Florida, was born on his family's farm in Hopewell, New York, on January 2, 1830. Seeing no future for himself in agriculture, he left home at age 14 — with nine cents in his pocket — to work in a relative's business in Ohio. Modest success in the 1850s prompted him to purchase a salt company in Saginaw, Michigan, but the firm went bankrupt after the Civil War. Undaunted, Flagler moved to Cleveland and joined forces with John D. Rockefeller, who needed help in expanding his fledging oil company. The two men, along with Samuel Andrews, formed Standard Oil in 1870 and made millions.

After his success in the oil business, Flagler turned to real estate. He had been spending winters in St. Augustine, Florida, because of his wife's poor health, and he saw great possibilities in developing the area for business and tourism. In 1888, he built the fabulous Ponce de Leon Hotel (now Flagler College) and several other hotels. To facilitate travel, he built railroads, and he developed land for business as well. Soon he had a Florida empire.

In 1881, his wife, Mary Harkness, died. Flagler married her nurse-companion, Alice Shourds, who became hopelessly insane and was institutionalized. Divorce followed, and then Flagler married Mary Lily Kenan of North Carolina. As a gift for his new bride, he hired John M. Carrère and Thomas Hastings, the architects who designed the U.S. Senate Building and the New York Public Library, to create a new home in Palm Beach. The real estate magnate wanted a noble Roman villa, befitting a man of his social standing, but he also loved the Spanish architecture of old St. Augustine. To accommodate both of his desires, Carrère and Hastings designed a Roman palace in marble with Spanish accents.

The 55-room three-story home, built on six acres of waterfront property, is fronted by a wide portico with Roman Doric columns.

In 1901, Henry Morrison Flagler married for the third time and built the palatial mansion Whitehall as a wedding gift for his new bride.

Two enormous urns, set on marble steps, flank the front entrance. The roof is red tile, a Spanish touch that Flagler found most pleasing.

The major rooms of the palace that Flagler called "Whitehall" are decorated and furnished to reflect Continental taste, mostly French, but American and British touches can also be found. The arched front door leads to a 110-by-40-foot marble entrance hall with its huge circular painted ceiling and impressive Ionic columns. In the back of the building is a magnificent ballroom, decorated in Louis XV style. The first floor also includes the music room, a billiard room, a dining room and kitchen, Flagler's office, a library, a French salon, and service rooms. In the center of the first floor is a large courtyard that resembles a lounging area for Roman statesmen.

The second-floor bedrooms are decorated in a variety of styles. One bedroom, used by Flagler's secretary, features wallpaper printed with yellow roses and matching bed covers and upholstery. Another reflects 20th-century English design. The "best" guest room features Louis XV decor. Flagler and his wife shared a rococo suite which includes separate dressing rooms and a marble-floored bathroom.

The Flaglers lived at Whitehall only from January through April. They spent most of the rest of the year at their home in Mamaroneck, New York. Flagler commuted between the two residences until his death in 1913. When his wife died four years later, the house passed to her niece, Louise Lewis. She sold it to a group of investors who converted it to a hotel and attached a 300-room tower to its west side. In 1959, when it had become too expensive to maintain as a hotel and was in danger of being destroyed, Jean Flagler Matthews, Flagler's granddaughter, instituted the Henry Morrison Flagler Museum, which bought the property and began the task of restoration, including severing Whitehall from the hotel tower to which it had been attached.

The restoration continues. Whitehall—also known as the Henry Morrison Flagler Museum—is open to visitors, and its ballroom is used for recitals and charitable affairs.

(Opposite top) The music room at Whitehall features an organ and piano. Mrs. Flagler was an accomplished singer and organist.

(Opposite bottom) Whitehall's bedrooms are furnished in a variety of styles; this one has ornate rococo furnishings.

The elegant room, decorated and furnished in the style of King Francis I, was the setting for formal dinners attended by guests such as John Jacob Astor, Woodrow Wilson, and the Vanderbilts.

We hold these truths to be self-evident, that all men are created equal, that they are endowed by their Creator with certain unalienable Rights, that among these are Life, Liberty and the pursuit of Happiness.

From the Declaration of Independence

Painting by Rembrandt Peale. New York Historical Society.

ONTICELLO is testimony to the brilliance of its creator, Thomas Jefferson, author of the Declaration of Independence, third President of the United States, architect of the University of Virginia, visionary statesman, writer, and scholar. To visit Jefferson's home, and to consider how it evolved over 40 years, is to begin to appreciate the well-organized mind of this genius.

Jefferson was born on his father's 1550-acre plantation near Charlottesville, Virginia, in 1743. When his father died 14 years later, the land was inherited by young Thomas. After receiving his education at William and Mary College, he decided to build a new home on a wooded hill of the estate and to call it "Monticello"—little mountain in Italian. He cleared the land and began to build in 1769.

Jefferson's plans called for a two-story house with a two-story columned portico built in the classical Roman style, a type of architecture which he preferred to that of the popular Georgian mansions of his day. Interestingly, his break with architectural forms imported from Great Britain foreshadowed his political break with the mother country several years later. For construction, he chose red bricks from Virginia, instead of stone or wood, which were used for many of the Commonwealth's plantation homes.

Jefferson, an avid reader, spent many relaxing hours in his first-floor library.

Instead of his era's popular Georgian style of architecture, Thomas Jefferson looked to classical Greek and Roman buildings as models for Monticello.

In 1771, when he married Martha Wayles Shelton, only one wing of the house and a small separate pavillion were completed. Even in 1782, at the time of Martha's death, the house was still under construction. Finally, in 1784, when Jefferson left for Europe, the two-tiered plan with a single-tiered porch lacked only the upper portico to reach its resolution. During the next 20 years, Jefferson's political activities kept him away from Monticello for long periods of time. He participated in two Continental Congresses and served as governor of Virginia during the War for Independence.

Jefferson began to redesign Monticello in 1793, having spent five years as a U.S. Minister to France, where he studied French neoclassical architecture. A man who absorbed and used what he read, whether it was political theory or architectural practice, Jefferson extensively remodeled his home employing some of the techniques he had seen and studied in Europe. A substantial addition was attached to the east side of the house, a staircase was removed, and an imposing dome was constructed above the central parlor on the west side. When he was finished remodeling in 1809, having served two terms in the White House during the interim, he had created one of the world's finest examples of neoclassical architecture.

The east portico leads to a large entrance hall and to the parlor at the west side of the house. The south wing contains Jefferson's personal suite — a bedroom two stories high, a

Jefferson's bed is tucked into an alcove
between his dressing room and his study,
giving him easy access to both rooms.

The furnishings throughout Monticello are
simple yet elegant.

library, and a study. Jefferson's bed is neatly
tucked into an alcove between the study and
bedroom, allowing him easy access to either
room. The north wing contains the two-story
dining room and adjacent tea room, where
Jefferson entertained statesmen and friends.
The stairways leading to the second-floor bedrooms and attics are narrow and are placed
out of sight; ever the pragmatist, Jefferson
thought that large stairways required too much
space. Throughout the house, the furniture
and decorations are simple and understated,
yet elegant.

Jefferson paid equal attention to the outbuildings and grounds. Underground pass-
ageways, covered by raised terraces, lead to
the outbuildings that flank the house—the kitchen and servants' quarters on the south side,
the stable and carriage house on the north.
Gardens and orchards surround the house.

Jefferson lived at his Monticello estate until his death on July 4, 1826, exactly 50 years
after he signed the Declaration of Independence. (His friend and cosigner, John Adams,
died the same day; see p.19.) The home remained in the family until 1831, when it was
sold. Although subsequent owners endeav-
ored to preserve Monticello, 1870 photo-
graphs show a then-unoccupied structure with
a rickety front gate, broken windows, crum-
bling steps, and weed-infested gutters. Fortu-
nately the mansion was stabilized by Jefferson
Monroe Levy in the 1880s. Then, in 1923, the
Thomas Jefferson Memorial Foundation purchased the house and began a more extensive
restoration. Today, the home on Virginia Highway 53 is splendidly restored and impeccably
maintained.

The Home of

Thomas Wolfe

1900–1938

I intend to wreak out my soul on paper and express it all. This is what my life means to me: I am at the mercy of this thing and I will do it or die.

When Mrs. Wolfe was running her boarding house, this living room was bustling with activity.

IN *LOOK HOMEWARD ANGEL*, the first of Thomas Wolfe's long autobiographical novels, Eliza Gant, the protagonist's mother, moves out of her family's home and buys an old boarding house called "Dixieland." Wolfe described it as "a big cheaply constructed frame house of eighteen or twenty drafty high-ceilinged rooms: it had a rambling, unplanned, gabular appearance, and was painted dirty yellow." It had a pleasant yard bordered by maple trees, but in winter, "the wind blew howling blasts under the skirts of Dixieland: its back end was built high off the ground on wet columns of rotting bricks." A small furnace warmed the first-floor rooms but gave the upstairs "a chill radiation."

In reality, Wolfe was describing the house at 48 Spruce Street in Asheville, North Carolina, a large Victorian with assorted balconies, angles, and gables that was named "Old Kentucky Home." Wolfe spent many of his childhood years there, and was buried in nearby Riverside Cemetery.

Like Eliza Gant, Thomas's mother left the family home on Woodfin Street in 1906 to pursue her interest in real estate. She took Tom with her and set up the Spruce Street boardinghouse. Young Thomas spent many less than happy years being shuffled from bedroom to bedroom as boarders moved in and out. Because the boarders filled the first-floor dining room at suppertime, Thomas and his brother had to eat off a marble-covered table in the pantry next to the kitchen. The boardinghouse parlor was cluttered with old furniture, and the upstairs bedrooms featured all the trimmings of a cheap hotel.

Though Wolfe disliked "Old Kentucky Home" and was glad to get away from it—to college at the University of North Carolina at Chapel Hill, to Harvard, to New York, to Europe seven times, and to the American West—the house and the life that swirled within and around it made a lasting mark on the developing writer. The unhappy boy in the unpleasant boarding house became the "lost" hero of his long novels, endlessly searching for his roots and concluding that "you can't go home again." Wolfe was arguably overshadowed by the literary giants of his generation—Ernest Hemingway, F. Scott Fitzgerald, William Faulkner—but few writers have provided a more accurate view of life in small-town America.

Wolfe died in 1939, before his 38th birthday. His mother continued to live in the Spruce Street house for many years. Today, the home is the site of the Thomas Wolfe Memorial.

The Home of

Joel Chandler Harris

c. 1848–1908

Brer Rabbit keep on axin' 'im, en de Tar-Baby, she keep on sayin' nothin,' twel present'y Brer Rabbit draw back wid his fis,' he did, in blip he tuck 'er side er de head.

From *Nights With Uncle Remus*

Photograph. c. 1906. Library of Congress.

THE RECENT popularity of traditional storytelling, inspired by monologuists like Spaulding Gray and Garrison Keillor, has reawakened interest in a great 19th-century storyteller, Joel Chandler Harris, author of the Uncle Remus tales that have entertained children and adults around the world. Harris lived the last 28 of his 60 years at The Wren's Nest, his Victorian residence at 1050 Gordon Street in Atlanta, Georgia.

What today is a sprawling Victorian home with a large Queen Anne facade and long porches was once a humble farmhouse. The original structure, built around 1871 by the Muse family, contained only a dining room and bedroom on the main floor (where they are today) and a kitchen in the basement. Five years later, the Muses made a substantial addition, attaching two bedrooms, a parlor, and a long hallway that now occupies the center of the house. Windows and doors were arranged to allow maximum cross-ventilation during hot Georgia summers. A small covered porch was added to the front of the house to shade the parlor windows and to provide an outdoor sitting area.

The Muses sold the house in the mid-1870s, and in 1881 it was purchased by Clark Howell, owner of the *Atlanta Constitution*. He leased the house to Harris, one of the paper's reporters; two years later, Harris bought the home. At the time he moved in, Harris had recently published *Uncle Remus: His Songs and Sayings*, tales of Br'er Rabbit and Br'er Bear. These stories were modeled after those Harris had heard as a child from plantation slaves.

Soon after he became the owner, Harris began to turn the modest farmhouse into a manor appropriate for a nationally-known literary figure. He added the noble Queen Anne facade, stretched the porch across the entire front of the house and around the side, attached a kitchen to the dining room, installed an upstairs bedroom, and expanded the ground floor.

The new rooms, tastefully decorated with mahogany-stained woodwork and new mantle pieces, included an entranceway and east and west parlors. The former parlor was converted to a study and library, where Harris wrote his stories. When the renovation was complete, Harris had the estate of a Southern literary

Stained-glass windows add color to the west parlor, which was added to the house in 1884. The room contains original Harris furnishings.

96

While Joel Chandler Harris lived at The Wren's Nest, he transformed the structure from a simple farmhouse to a rambling Victorian home.

gentleman. From his comfortable Atlanta nest, he wrote many of the more than 30 books that he published during his lifetime.

Around 1900, when Harris retired from the *Atlanta Constitution*, he altered his home one last time to bring it into the 20th century. He installed indoor plumbing and a bathroom and wired the house for electricity. After that, he made no more changes.

Harris died in 1908, and five years later his widow sold the home to the Uncle Remus Memorial Association, which kept it as a museum. Since 1983, The Wren's Nest has been managed by the Joel Chandler Harris Association, which has raised funds for its restoration. Today, visitors can view the home and enjoy the performances of local storytellers who use it as their forum.

Helen Keller

1880–1968

It were far better to sail forever in the night of blindness with sense, and feeling, and mind, than to be content with the mere act of seeing. The only lightless dark is the night of darkness in ignorance and insensibility.

From an article in *Reader's Digest,* August 1952

Photograph. c. 1920. Library of Congress.

IN 1820, Helen's grandfather, built a Virginia-style 1½-story house on his 640-acre cotton farm in Tuscumbia, Alabama. It is a modest structure with four downstairs rooms—a bedroom and parlor in the front and a dining room and bedroom in the back. There are also two upstairs bedrooms and a trunk, or storage, room. Like many Southern homes, it has the kitchen out back to protect the main house from fire and from heat during the long Alabama summers. The house was called "Ivy Green" because of the ivy growing alongside.

Sometime later, Keller added another building to his modest estate, a small office near the house where he could keep the plantation's books. Later, as the family grew, the small office was expanded and turned into a bedroom for Keller's sons. When one of the sons, Arthur, brought his new wife, Kate Adams Keller, to Ivy Green, the small building was arranged as a bridal suite for the young couple. Helen Keller was born in that suite on June 27, 1880.

She was a healthy child until she was almost two years old. Then a sudden illness struck, leaving her unable to see or hear, and she quickly forgot the few words she had learned to speak. For the next five years, she lived in an insulated world, unable to communicate or interact with her family. When she was almost seven, her parents brought Anne Sullivan of the Perkins Institute in Boston to Ivy Green to work with Helen. Sullivan, only 19 years old, turned out to be the miracle worker who broke through the child's wall of silence.

Teacher and pupil lived in the office to the side of the house. One of the building's two rooms was a bedroom, the other a playroom and, in a sense, the schoolroom where Sullivan tried to teach Helen to recognize words by tapping out an alphabetic code on the child's hand. The lessons were frustrating for both teacher and pupil, but one day, near the well pump in the yard, Sullivan reached her student by running water on one of the child's hands and taping out the word "water" in code on the other.

After that initial breakthrough, progress was steady. In two years, Helen was reading books recorded in Braille and learning to

This is a view of the Keller home at Ivy Green from the cottage near the house.

After Helen learned to read Braille, she became an avid reader and writer.

99

The Kellers' parlor and dining room (in background) are furnished with
pieces from the early 1800s.

write with a typewriter. At age 10, she wanted to learn to speak and was sent to Horace Mann School for the Deaf in Boston, where she developed an understandable voice. After attending the Cambridge School for Young Ladies, she gained admission to Radcliffe College and graduated cum laude in 1904. Sullivan continued working with Helen through her college years, using code to spell her teachers' lectures into Helen's hand. The two women also collaborated on Keller's autobiography, *The Story of My Life*.

After college, Keller began touring in the United States and overseas, giving lectures, translated to audiences by Sullivan, on the necessity of providing educational and work opportunities for people who could not see, hear, or speak. Often in those days, people with such handicaps were classified as "idiots," and Keller's lectures helped to change those notions. She also became a spokeswoman for the women's rights movement.

Keller never returned permanently to Ivy Green. In the 1930s, she and Sullivan moved to a home in Connecticut provided by the American Foundation. Sullivan died in 1936, but after World War II, Keller, almost 70 years old, made another world tour to speak on behalf of the blind. She died in Westport, Connecticut, in 1968. Her burial urn is housed next to that of Anne Sullivan in the National Cathedral in Washington, D.C.

In 1954, through the efforts of the Helen Keller Property Board and the State of Alabama, Ivy Green was established as a permanent memorial to Helen Keller and placed on the National Register of Historic Places. Today, visitors can tour the home and attend the Helen Keller Festival, held each June. From the end of June through July, William Gibson's Pulitzer Prize—winning play about Helen and her gifted teacher, *The Miracle Worker*, is performed on the grounds of Ivy Green.

At this well pump, Anne Sullivan broke through Helen Keller's wall of silence by tapping out *w-a-t-e-r* in code on one of the child's hands and running water over the other hand.

Helen's bedroom at Ivy Green is simply but tastefully decorated with functional furniture, a wood floor covered with a patterned carpet, and white ruffled curtains.

The Home of
Jefferson Davis
1808–1889

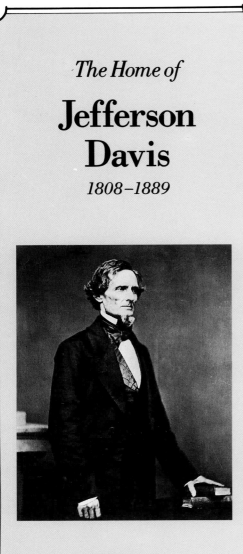

I worked night and day for twelve years to prevent war, but I could not. . . . Now it must go on until the last man of this generation falls in his tracks and his children seize his musket and fight our battles.

From his statement to President Lincoln's emissaries, April 17, 1864

Photograph by the Washburn Studio. Library of Congress.

The parlor at Beauvoir contains some of the Davises' original furnishings. A portrait of the Confederate leader, the last painted before his death, hangs above the handsome fireplace.

N 1877, JEFFERSON DAVIS, President of the Confederate States of America, was a man without a home. Since the South's defeat in the Civil War, he had spent two years in federal custody at Fort Monroe, Virginia (accused but never convicted of helping to plot Abraham Lincoln's assassination). He had also traveled in Canada, Britain, and continental Europe; and taken up temporary living quarters in Memphis, Tennessee. His prewar estate, Brierfield, near Vicksburg, Mississippi, had been lost, and he had little money with which to establish another. A lifelong friend, Sarah Dorsey, invited him to board at her estate, Beauvoir, on the Gulf Coast in Biloxi, Mississippi, and Davis accepted her invitation. He would call Beauvoir home for the rest of his life.

Davis was an honorable man who did not deserve the life of a wandering, rootless wayfarer. A West Point graduate, he served his country well in the Black Hawk War and the Mexican War. He represented Mississippi in the House of Representatives and the Senate and held the office of Secretary of War in President Franklin Pierce's cabinet. When his home state seceded from the Union, however, he resigned his Senate seat and worked for the Confederate cause. On February 18, 1861, he was inaugurated as President of the Confederacy, an office he held until the end of the Civil War. After the South's defeat, he was seen by Northerners not as a retired statesman but as a rebel and outlaw.

Mrs. Dorsey's invitation was a gift from the gods. Her splendid home overlooking a sandy beach on the Gulf Coast was a symbol of the antebellum South, the attempted preservation of which had cost Davis his career. Built in the late 1840s or early 1850s as a summer retreat by James Brown, a wealthy planter from Madison County, Mississippi, it afforded Davis a home in the style to which he had been accustomed. A columned porch wraps around the

Twelve years after the Civil War, Jefferson Davis found peace in this splendid Mississippi home overlooking the Gulf of Mexico.

103

front and sides of the elevated house, allowing an unobstructed view of the Gulf of Mexico. Inside, a wide central receiving hall, running the width of the house and capturing the cool water breezes, connects two downstairs bedrooms and two parlors. At the rear are two extensions, connected by a back porch, containing two additional bedrooms as well as a dining room and a butler's pantry.

Initially Davis and his family occupied one of the two small pavilions that flank the main house. Seeing that Davis was so delighted with life at Beauvoir, Mrs. Dorsey sold him the estate for a token sum. Davis, his wife, Varina, and their younger daughter, Winnie, moved into the main house. He took a rear bedroom that offered a water view and used his former living quarters in the small pavilion to the right of the house as a study where he worked on the projects that would occupy him in his retirement—the writing of *The Rise and Fall of the Confederate Government* and *A Short History of the Confederate States of America.*

Davis died in New Orleans on December 6, 1889. After his death, Varina Davis and her daughter, Winnie, moved to New York but struggled to keep Beauvoir through financial hardships. Mrs. Davis refused a $90,000 offer for the estate from a developer who wanted to turn it into a hotel and eventually sold it for $10,000 to the Mississippi Division of the United Sons of Confederate Veterans. From 1904 through 1957, Beauvoir was used as the Jefferson Davis Home for Confederate Soldiers and Sailors. In 1924, a hospital was built on the estate a short distance from the house for the care of ill Confederate veterans and their wives or widows. In 1941, Beauvoir was opened to the public as the Jefferson Davis Shrine. In 1978, a bill restoring Davis's citizenship (which he relinquished during the Civil War) passed the U.S. Congress without a dissenting vote and was signed by President Jimmy Carter.

Today, visitors can tour the last home of Jefferson Davis as well as the Davis Family Museum, built under the living quarters, and the Confederate Museum in what was once the hospital. Also on the grounds is the Tomb of the Unknown Soldier of the Confederate States.

The stylishly furnished bedroom at Beauvoir provided Davis with a view of the Gulf of Mexico.

In his library in the small pavillion to the right of the main house, Davis wrote *The Rise and Fall of the Confederate Government.*

The Home of

John Ringling

1866–1936

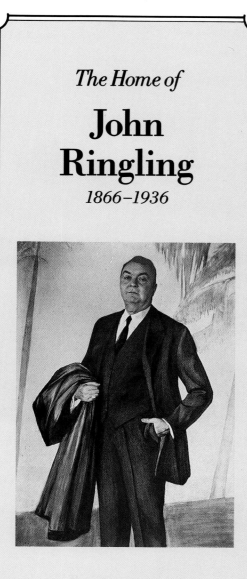

I thought people needed to laugh more this year than ever. . . . I tried to make the show funnier so people could forget their troubles.

On the 1932 edition of the Ringling Brothers Barnum & Bailey Circus

Painting by Savely Sorine. c. 1927. The John and Mable Ringling Museum of Art.

JOHN RINGLING WAS the son of a harness maker, a German immigrant, from Baraboo, Wisconsin. In 1884, when John was 18 years old, he and his brothers started a two-animal circus that traveled by wagon. By 1900, they had the largest circus in the country. In 1919, they bought out the Barnum & Bailey Circus, forming what eventually came to be known as "the greatest show on earth."

In 1924, Ringling and his wife, Mabel, decided to build a mansion overlooking the bay on their vacation estate in Sarasota, Florida. The Ringlings commissioned Dwight James Baum of New York to create a palace that would combine features from two of Mrs. Ringling's favorite buildings—the Doge's Palace in Venice and the old Madison Square Garden in New York, where the circus often performed. The Ringlings then began a European tour to purchase accessories for their new home.

These were the roaring twenties, and the home that Baum completed in 1926 is a tribute to the opulence of the age. The two-story mansion is 200 feet long, with a 60-foot-high square tower that rises above the red-tiled roof. The pale-pink building is trimmed with multicolored terra-cotta accents, suggestive of a Venetian palace. The house was named "Ca' d'Zan," meaning "House of John" in patois.

Inside, the front door leads to the huge two-story living room, patterned after an Italian Renaissance courtyard and decorated with reproductions of Louis XIV, XV, and XVI period furniture. Spreading out from the living room are more than 30 other rooms, decorated in reproductions of European (primarily French) styles. John's large second-floor bedroom resembles the sleeping quarters of a European emperor, and the large tower above the home is a Turkish-style kiosk with profuse terra-cotta decorations. Outside the home are marble terraces, ornate balustrades, and exotic gardens.

Unfortunately, Mrs. Ringling enjoyed the home for less than three years. She died in 1929, at age 54. Several years later, John Ringling experienced serious financial reverses which ultimately cost him the management of his circus. He died in 1936, deeding Ca' d'Zan, and his private art collection—housed in an Italian-Renaissance-style villa—to the state of Florida. Most of the home's furniture and its decorations remain in place. An 18th-century Italianate court playhouse, the Asolo Theater, and Circus Galleries were later added on the grounds of the estate.

Ca' d'Zan, John Ringling's pale-pink palace, overlooks Sarasota Bay.

Cedar Hill, Frederick Douglass's estate in the southeastern part of Washington, D.C., is set on a high hill overlooking the Anacostia River.

FREDERICK DOUGLASS was born a slave on a plantation in Talbot County, Maryland, in about 1818. When he was about 18 years of age, his owner rented him to a shipbuilder in Baltimore, where he mingled with free blacks and became literate. Two years later, he escaped from slavery and fled to New York and freedom. Eventually he married Anna Murray and settled in New Bedford, Massachusetts, where he became active in the abolitionist movement. In 1845, he published his autobiography, *Narrative of the Life of Frederick Douglass, An American Slave.*

After the Civil War, Douglass became a leading spokesman in the movement to secure civil rights for recently freed slaves. He advised political leaders, wrote and lectured on issues that affected black Americans, and held important administrative posts in Washington, D.C.

In 1877, having lived in Washington for almost five years, Douglass purchased Cedar Hill, a 9¾-acre estate in the southeastern part of the city. The estate is a perfect reflection of the man who had risen from slavery to become a nationally known figure of the highest rank.

Cedar Hill sits on a high crest overlooking the Anacostia River and the U.S. Capitol, a prestigious location that suggests Douglass's own position in the Washington community. The area had been zoned for whites only, and the original owner of the estate had stipulated that the land should never be sold to blacks; that impediment, like other barriers in Douglass's life, was overcome. The house that sits on the center of the estate is a fine Victorian home of some 20 rooms with a handsome columned porch stretching across its front, an appropriate forum from which a leading statesman could address his followers.

The house served as both home and office. The east side of the first floor contains a parlor, used by Douglass as a reception area, and a library of some 1000 volumes, where Douglass did most of his writing. The west side of the first floor is the family living area, consisting of a parlor and dining room. In the rear of the house are a kitchen, pantry, and service rooms. Pictures of Douglass's contemporaries—

A columned porch spans the front of the Douglass home, offering spectacular sunsets.

Abraham Lincoln, Susan B. Anthony, and others — are hung throughout the house.

In keeping with the Victorian custom, the second floor contains separate bedrooms for Douglass and his wife, as well as sleeping quarters for male and female guests. The small attic rooms were, in Douglass's time, set up to accommodate his 21 grandchildren, who were frequent visitors.

The house is surrounded by cedars, hickories, and oaks. Douglass enjoyed walking and working outdoors, and the estate offered him ample opportunities. A short distance from the house is a one-room stone building which Douglass used as a study when the house became too noisy.

Douglass lived his last 17 years at Cedar Hill, enjoying the fresh air, the five-mile walk to downtown Washington, and the frequent visitors. After his death in 1895, Helen Pitts Douglass, his second wife, organized the Frederick Douglass Memorial and Historical Association, which worked with the national Association of Colored Women's Clubs to open the home to visitors, a goal which was achieved in 1916. Since 1962, the National Park Service has maintained the Frederick Douglass National Historic Site, which is credited by the American Association of Museums.

The east parlor features a leather rocking chair from Haiti. The table and lamp were gifts from Senator Charles Sumner of Massachusetts.

The Home of

George Washington Vanderbilt

1862–1914

Mr. Vanderbilt has more workers and a larger budget for his forestry projects than I have at my disposal for the whole Department of Agriculture.

From a statement by J. Sterling Morton, U.S. Secretary of Agriculture,

Painting by John Singer Sargent. c. 1900. The Biltmore Estate.

O F ALL THE HOMES designed for the Vanderbilt family by Richard Morris Hunt, the American architect schooled in the French Beaux Arts style, the most impressive is Biltmore House, home of George Washington Vanderbilt in Asheville, North Carolina. Cornelius's The Breakers (see pp. 32–35), William's Marble House, and Frederick's Hyde Park estate (see pp. 70–73) were "cottages" of 70 or 80 rooms. Biltmore House is one of America's largest dwellings, a majestic château of 250 rooms, built on a foundation that covers four acres.

During the late 1880s, George Washington Vanderbilt, a student of architecture and an art collector, often vacationed in the North Carolina mountains. He fell in love with a piece of land near Mt. Pisgah and began buying huge parcels, eventually owning almost 125,000 acres. In 1890, he commissioned Hunt to build a suitable country home on the land to house his valuable art collection.

Hunt designed a 16th-century French château, similar to the ones in the Loire Valley in France. The 780-foot-long edifice of Indiana limestone and its surrounding estate resemble a feudal manor. The building is asymmetrical, with high towers and ornately decorated facades, and with wings and pavilions jutting out from the large central tower. It took five years to complete and required the services of hundreds of laborers and craftsmen. A special railroad had to be built to transport construction materials to the North Carolina site. Vanderbilt named the estate "Biltmore" for the Dutch town, Bildt, where the family originated, and the English word, "more," meaning rolling hills.

A visitor enters the château through a large entrance hallway with a winding staircase leading to the upper levels. Beyond the entrance hall is a sunken indoor garden filled with palms and flowers. The most impressive room on the main floor is the 72-by-42-foot

George Washington Vanderbilt's 250-room home in Asheville, North Carolina, resembles a French château.

The 72-by-42-foot dining hall is an appropriate setting for a medieval royal banquet.

medieval banquet hall with a triple fireplace and 2 large chandeliers hanging from its 70-foot ceiling. The colorful flags suggest an eating hall in the court of some medieval French monarch, as do the statues of Joan of Arc and St. Louis above the doorway, and the moose and elk heads affixed to the walls. Other rooms of interest on the main floor include a library with two-tiered bookshelves, a gallery of valuable paintings and large tapestries, and a "gentlemen's quarters" containing a billiard room, smoking room, and trophy room.

The second-floor bedrooms and guest rooms are decorated in a variety of styles. Edith Vanderbilt's bedroom features rococo furniture of the Louis XV period. An oak sitting room is tastefully decorated in 17th-century Jacobean. G. W. Vanderbilt's room is outfitted with 17th-to-19th-century Spanish, Italian, and Portuguese furniture, as well as American pieces designed by Richard Morris Hunt. A guest room is done in Chippendale.

The lower level of Biltmore is devoted to sports and games. A Halloween room is arranged for informal parties, and a Brunswick bowling alley, swimming pool, and gymnasium provided indoor exercise for Biltmore's guests. Also on the lower floors are living quarters for dozens of servants, three separate kitchens, and laundry rooms.

Most Biltmore visitors also explore the grounds and outbuildings. The centerpiece of the carefully manicured grounds, designed by Frederick Law Olmstead, is the 4-acre English walled garden, one of America's finest, with conservatory and greenhouses. Nearby are the stables, carriage houses, and the Biltmore Estate Winery. The home is surrounded by thousands of acres of woods and rolling hills, once stocked with game for the Vanderbilts' guests to hunt and still carefully managed.

Vanderbilt used Biltmore as his private residence until his death in 1914. Soon afterward, his wife, Edith, deeded part of the estate to the government to create Pisgah National Forest. In 1930, his daughter, Mrs. Cornelia Cecil, and her husband opened Biltmore and its gardens to visitors. The mansion, the artworks within, and the surrounding gardens and forests are carefully preserved as a tribute to the Gilded Age and its bygone way of life.

Biltmore's library has two tiers of books and a large fireplace with a splendid mantel.

Beyond Biltmore's entrance hall is a sunken indoor garden covered by a glass dome.

The Home of
Robert E. Lee
1807–1870

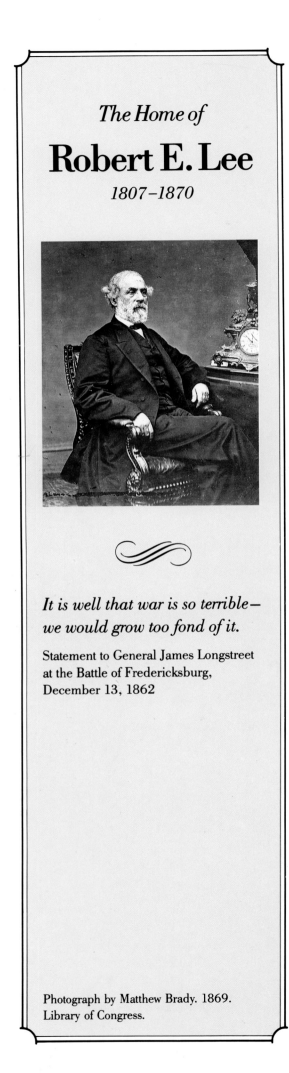

*It is well that war is so terrible—
we would grow too fond of it.*

Statement to General James Longstreet
at the Battle of Fredericksburg,
December 13, 1862

Photograph by Matthew Brady. 1869.
Library of Congress.

ARLINGTON HOUSE, now the Robert E. Lee Memorial, was actually the home of Lee's wife's family. It was built by George Washington Parke Custis, the grandson of Martha Washington by her first marriage to Daniel Parke Custis. G. W. P. Custis and his wife, Mary, had only one child who survived infancy—Mary Anna, whom Lee married at Arlington House in 1831. Lee, a West Point graduate, had come from an old Virginia family that included two signers of the Declaration of Independence. Lee's father, Gen. Henry ("Light Horse Harry") Lee, was a Revolutionary War hero and later Governor of Virginia.

The house that G. W. P. Custis began in 1802 and completed in 1817 is a splendid mansion in the neoclassical style. It was built on the hill of the 1100-acre Custis estate and offers a clear view of the Potomac River. The large central portion is fronted by a portico and eight massive columns and is flanked by two large single-story wings. George Hadfield, the architect, might have modeled the house after an ancient Athenian temple, Theseum.

Inside, Arlington House was arranged to suit the needs of a large Virginia family. A central hallway connects the large White Parlor on one side to a less formal family parlor and dining room on the other. The south wing holds a morning room, Custis's office and studio, and a conservatory. The north wing includes a pantry, bath, and guest chambers. Upstairs are the Lee family bed rooms. The Lees had seven chidlren, six born at Arlington House.

Robert E. Lee considered Arlington House home after his marriage to Mary Anna, and the couple lived there for 30 years, though Lee's military assignments often took them away from Virginia. He was, for example, superintendent of West Point from 1852 to 1855.

With the outbreak of the Civil War, President Lincoln offered Lee command of a large Union army that was to take the field against the rebel forces of Virginia. He refused because he felt it was his duty to follow his beloved state and fight on the side of the Confederacy. As commander of the Army of Northern Virginia and later general-in-chief of the Con-

The Lees' four
daughters used this
second-floor chamber
as a playroom and
dressing room.

(Opposite) Arlington
House was originally
the home of the
Custises, the family
of Gen. Robert E.
Lee's wife.

federate armies, he distinguished himself in numerous engagements, often against numerically superior forces. Indeed, the sight of the erect, white-haired Lee astride his grey horse Traveller became an almost mythic image to the South.

During the Civil War, the home was held by Union forces and eventually confiscated. When the war ended, Lee accepted the post of president at Washington College in Lexington, Virginia, and he lived there until his death in 1870. Twelve years later, Lee's son, George Washington Custis Lee, won a suit against the government to regain possession of Arlington House. He accepted $150,000 in lieu of the estate, a portion of which had already been used to create Arlington National Cemetery. In 1925, the War Department began restoring the mansion under the direction of the U.S. Congress. In 1933, President Franklin D. Roosevelt transfered the responsibility for continuing the restoration to the National Park Service. In 1974, Congress restored the name Arlington House to the estate in honor of the Confederate General.

A portrait of Mrs. Lee hangs over the fireplace in the family parlor.

And something about Cross Creek suits us—or something about us makes us cling to it contentedly, lovingly and often in exasperation, through the vicissitudes that have driven others away.

From *Cross Creek*

Photograph. c. 1935–42. University of Florida Library. Rare Books Collection.

Marjorie did most of her writing at this table in the screened-in front porch. At Cross Creek, she wrote *The Yearling*, her Pulitzer Prize–winning novel, and other works.

W HEN CHOOSING a locale for their stories and novels, writers often return to their native grounds. William Faulkner (see pp. 80–82), for example, developed his best fiction around the small Mississippi town where he spent most of his life. John Steinbeck's great novels and stories are set in his native Salinas Valley. The best work of Marjorie Kinnan Rawlings, however, is set not in the land of her birth but in the scrub country of central Florida, the home she adopted when she was 32 years old.

Marjorie Kinnan was born in 1896 in Washington, D.C., and attended the University of Wisconsin, graduating in 1918 with a major in English. A year later, she married Charles Rawlings, a college classmate, and the couple moved to Rochester, New York, where they worked as newspaper reporters.

Charles's two brothers lived in Island Grove in central Florida, and in 1928 the Rawlingses, wishing to find a quiet place to write and hoping to engage in a joint project to improve their faltering marriage, bought a 74-acre citrus farm in the small community of Cross Creek, near Island Grove. They named their new homestead "Los Hermanos"—which, in Spanish, means "The Brothers"—in honor of the two men who helped them move in and work the farm.

The house on Los Hermanos, built in the 1890s, is actually three separate buildings. They were probably constructed at different times and are connected by enclosed porches and breezeways in an example of the "cracker"-style farmhouse that was common in the rural South around the turn of the century. Like most cracker houses, the Rawlingses' dwelling, built for the hot, humid climate, had separate units for the main residence, for cooking and eating rooms, and for sleeping quarters; this design kept cooking heat away from the living area and allowed for maximum cross-ventilation during the long Florida summers. Roof overhangs shade the interior from the hot midday sun.

Surrounding the house is an Eden of citrus, palm, and oak trees. The Rawlingses hired farmhands. Like other Florida citrus farmers, they raised vegetables for their own table, battled winter frosts, and bartered to get a good price for their produce.

But Marjorie's real work in Cross Creek was writing. In the enclosed front porch, she began to create stories about the landscape and people —"crackers," they were often derisively called — of her new community. In 1930, she sold her first Florida sketch, "Cracker Chidlings," to *Scribner's* magazine. Encouraged by that success, she began work on her first novel, *South Moon Under*, published in 1933. That same year, Marjorie and Charles were divorced, but she continued to live at Cross Creek and write about the local folks to whom she had become so attached. In 1938, she published *The Yearling*, her third novel, which deals with a young boy's coming-of-age in the Ocala scrub, a wilderness area 35 miles from Cross Creek, surrounding Orange Lake. The novel earned her a Pulitzer Prize and national recognition. During the next several years, she penned the autobiographical *Cross Creek*, several more novels, and one of her most popular books, *Cross Creek Cookery*.

In 1941, Marjorie married Norton Baskin, a hotel owner, and moved to his penthouse in the Castle Warden Hotel in St. Augustine, Florida. Several years later, the Baskins purchased a farm in Van Hornesville, New York, and lived in Florida only during the winter months. But Marjorie continued to write Cross Creek stories until her death in 1953. She is buried in a cemetery near Island Grove.

After her death, the Cross Creek estate was willed to the University of Florida. The home was restored and opened to the public in 1970, under the auspices of the Florida Park Service.

Marjorie Kinnan Rawlings's Cross Creek home consists of three separate buildings connected by enclosed porches and breezeways — an example of the Southern "cracker" farmhouse.

Poets Robert Frost and Wallace Stevens were among the guests who used this bedroom; the antique spool bed was given to Rawlings by a Florida historian.

The kitchen cupboard holds oranges and grapefruits grown on the Cross Creek farm.

The Home of
Martin Luther King, Jr.
1929–1968

MARTIN LUTHER KING, JR., America's greatest civil rights leader, was born on January 15, 1929, in a pleasant Queen Anne Victorian house at 501 Auburn Avenue in Atlanta, Georgia. The house was built in 1894 and purchased in 1909 by the Reverend A. D. Williams, King's maternal grandfather. At the time of Martin's birth, it sheltered a large extended family including King's maternal grandparents, his parents, his older brother, and occasionally other relations.

The two-story house with a front porch and large gable contains five downstairs rooms connected by a central hallway—a front parlor, a dining room, a kitchen and work area, a bedroom, and a study where the minister prepared for his Sunday sermons at nearby Ebenezer Baptist Church.

Martin Luther King, Jr., was born in his parents' bedroom on the second floor of the house. As a child, Martin shared a room with his younger brother, Alfred, born in 1930. The other second-floor bedrooms were used by other family members and student boarders.

In this comfortable family home, Martin lived much like other Atlanta youngsters. He completed his school lessons and household chores, avoided piano practice, and teased his older sister. Although the neighborhood was virtually all black and schools were segregated, he often played with the son of a white grocer whose store was across the street. At night, he listened to his grandfather and father, also a minister, read from the Bible and lead the family in prayer. His parents and grandparents stressed the importance of family unity, personal pride, hard work, and faith in God—values that Martin would carry with him for the rest of his life.

In 1941, after the deaths of the Reverend and Mrs. Williams, Martin's parents moved to a larger brick home a few blocks away. During the next several years, the young King completed grade school and high school—he skipped two years because of good grades—and graduated from Morehouse College. Like his grandfather and father, he attended a seminary and then served as a minister at Ebenezer Baptist Church. He subsequently received his Ph.D. in systematic theology from Boston University. He met his future wife, Coretta Scott, in Boston. They were married in 1953.

Dr. King's civil rights work began when he moved to Montgomery, Alabama, in 1954 to accept a pastorate. There he became the leader of the Montgomery Improvement Association, which spearheaded the city's bus boycott. In 1960, he returned to Atlanta to start the Southern Christian Leadership Conference, the organization which, in 1963, promoted the Birmingham protests and the March on Washington, where Dr. King delivered his famous "I Have A Dream" speech.

Dr. King was assassinated on April 4, 1968, in Memphis, Tennessee. Three years later, his mother deeded the Auburn Avenue home to the Martin Luther King, Jr., Center in Atlanta. In 1980, the residential community in which Dr. King was born, with the surrounding commercial district, was designated a national park and is now administered by the National Park Service.

Martin Luther King, Jr., America's greatest civil rights leader, was born in a second-floor bedroom in this two-story middle-class home on Auburn Avenue in Atlanta.

George Washington

1732–1799

Let us therefore animate and encourage each other, and show the whole world that a Freeman, contending for liberty on his own, is superior to any slavish mercenary on earth.

From his general orders,
New York headquarters,
April 2, 1776

Painting by Rembrandt Peale. 1795.
Library of Congress.

LIKE HIS HOME, George Washington was commanding yet modest. By training he was a surveyor and soldier; by preference, a farmer. When named commander in chief of the Continental army in 1775, he was unsure of his fitness for command, even though he had served heroically in the French and Indian War. At the end of the Revolution he spurned attempts to make him a monarch and in 1789, accepted the presidency reluctantly but with the same strong commitment to public service that had always distinguished his career. Historians generally agree that without Washington's presence, the Revolution and the American experiment in constitutional government might not have succeeded.

Mount Vernon, a large Georgian mansion with a high columned porch that overlooks the Potomac River, testifies to its owner's quiet dignity and subtle elegance. The original house, built by George's father, Augustine Washington, about 1735, was much smaller than the present house. It consisted of 1½ stories and included a parlor and passage, dining room, and bed chambers. By 1754 George Washington had acquired the property by release from the widow of his elder half brother, Lawrence Washington. At her death in 1761, George came into full possession of the estate. His expansion program began in 1757 when he added a full story to his father's house, thus raising the height to its present 2½ stories. Additions in the 1770s added space at either end of the central block. He redid interior spaces, added outbuildings at the front connected by colonnades to the house, and improved the gardens and grounds. The familiar piazza was added to the back of the mansion in 1776, and the handsome cupola, in 1778. The cypress roof shingles were cut and painted to resemble clay tiles.

While much of this work was taking place, Washington was away on military affairs. He could not return to Mount Vernon until 1783, after the peace treaty was signed with Great Britain and he had given up his commission in the Continental army. Six years later, he was called away again for eight years to serve as the new nation's first President.

After leaving office in 1797, he retired to Mount Vernon for good. His home was now a fitting place for a former head of state. It had seven first-floor rooms connected by a central passage, which was paneled and painted, or grained, to resemble mahogany. The north side holds two parlors and a dining room suitable for large gatherings. On the opposite side are a small but formal dining room, a pantry, a bedroom, and a study, where Washington busied himself with his extensive correspondence. Upstairs are six bedrooms with two

The west entrance faces a dirt path where horses and carriages could approach the house.

The columned porch on George Washington's Mount Vernon home overlooks the Potomac River.

The west parlor was used for small, informal gatherings. The table is set for afternoon tea.

(Below right) Martha Washington's daughter, Nelly Custis, played the harpsichord in this small family parlor.

more bedrooms in the garret. Mount Vernon also contains over a dozen outbuildings, including a kitchen, a stable, a smoke house, slave quarters, and a large brick greenhouse.

Washington enjoyed only two years of retirement at this splendid estate. He died in 1799, and his wife, Martha, died three years later. Both are entombed at Mount Vernon. The Washingtons themselves were childless, although Mrs. Washington had children by her first marriage, and the estate passed to George Washington's nephew, Bushrod Washington, and eventually to *his* nephew, John Augustine Washington, III. In 1853, Ann Pamela Cunningham of South Carolina founded the Mount Vernon Ladies' Association, which purchased the home and about 200 of the estate's 8000 acres from John A. Washington, III, in 1859. The association continues to maintain Mount Vernon, which draws more than 1 million visitors each year.

The Central States

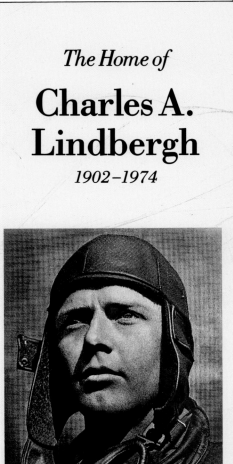

I heard a buzzing in the sky, and I climbed out a dormer window onto the roof and saw this winged machine soaring in the sky. It seemed wonderful and magical to me.

Photoengraving by Campbell Bros., New York. 1928. Library of Congress.

Charles Lindbergh's boyhood home, completed in 1906, replaced a larger Lindbergh home that burned to the ground a year earlier.

AMERICA'S greatest aviator, Charles A. Lindbergh, was born in Detroit in 1902 but raised on his parents' farm in Little Falls, Minnesota. One Lindbergh biographer claimed that young Charles had a Huckleberry Finn boyhood; he spent most of his time outdoors, romping through the woods and swimming in the Mississippi River and in Pike Creek.

The Lindbergh home now standing on the 110-acre Little Falls farm is the second dwelling at that location. The first, called "Lindholm," was a handsome 13-room home that Charles A. Lindbergh, Sr., an attorney, built in 1901. It burned to the ground four years later, and Mr. Lindbergh built a smaller 10-room house on its foundation.

The new home was used primarily as a summer bungalow. After Mr. Lindbergh was elected to the House of Representatives, where he served for a decade, the family spent winters in Washington, D.C., but in the summer, Mrs. Lindbergh and young Charles would return to Little Falls.

The two-story gabled house is modest, compared to the impressive one that burned down, but it suited Charles and his mother perfectly. The first floor contains a kitchen, a living room with Mrs. Lindbergh's piano, a small dining room, a sewing room, a bathroom, and two bedrooms. Off of the dining room is a screened-in porch which young Charles used as a bedroom in summer and winter. He kept a cot in one corner, and on cold Minnesota nights he put on his father's fur-lined coat, wrapped himself and his dog in blankets, and enjoyed the frigid air.

For several years, the second floor was unfinished and Charles used it as a playroom. When his father's political career ended and the family lived in Little Falls year round, it was converted to two bedrooms and a family room.

But young Charles spent more time outdoors than inside the house. He built a playhouse in the woods and passed many hours there. He learned to shoot a gun at an early age and to hunt fowl. His chores included hauling ice blocks to the icehouse for use in the kitchen. When he was 16 years old, his father turned the management of the farm over to him, and he increased its production, raising chickens, sheep, cattle, and hogs.

In 1920, Charles left the farm for the University of Wisconsin, where he majored in engineering. But since his boyhood he had been fascinated by aviation. In 1922, he left college to enroll in a Nebraska flight school.

After he learned to fly, Lindbergh joined the U.S. Army as a flying cadet. He graduated top man in his class and was commissioned a second lieutenant in the Army Air Service Reserve in 1925. He flew airmail routes and began to set air records, first from Chicago to St. Louis, then from San Diego to New York. On May 20, 1927, he attempted the impossible—a nonstop solo New York-to-Paris flight. As citizens on both sides of the Atlantic Ocean waited and prayed, Lindbergh flew his plane, the *Spirit of St. Louis*, over choppy seas for 33½ hours, landing in Paris to the cheers of thousands of onlookers. The flight made him an international hero.

He never returned to the farm. His father had died in 1924. His mother moved to Detroit to teach school, and the house remained vacant for several years. After the New York–Paris flight, souvenir hunters flocked to his boyhood home and helped themselves to some of the family keepsakes. Four years later, Charles, his mother, and his half sister Eva donated the house to the State of Minnesota as a memorial to Charles, Sr.

Lindbergh remained in aviation for the rest of his life, serving as a consultant and adviser to businesses and the armed forces. He also became interested in medicine, rocketry, and conservation and served on the World Wildlife Board of Trustees. In 1954, he was awarded a commission as brigadier general in the U.S. Air Force Reserve. He died in Hawaii in 1974, at age 72.

In 1969, the Lindbergh farm came under the management of the Minnesota Historical Society. The society also administers the nearby Lindberg Interpretive Center, built in 1972 to serve as a Lindbergh museum.

(Previous pages) **A hand-carved log is set above the field stone fireplace in the downstairs field room of Henry Ford's home in Dearborn, Michigan. The inscription—"Chop your own wood and it will warm you twice"—is a paraphrase of a line from Henry David Thoreau's *Walden*. (see pp. 138-141)**

Mrs. Land, Charles' maternal grandmother, used this bedroom every August when she vacationed with the Lindberghs. Grandmother Land died in this room in January 1919.

The Lindberghs ate most of their meals in the kitchen or on the screened-in porch, but the dining room, pictured here, was used for entertaining important guests. The china cabinet in the background holds dishes hand painted by Mrs. Lindbergh.

This carefully restored 1916 Saxon Six automobile is housed in the garage at the Lindbergh home. At age 14, Charles drove this car to California for a vacation with his mother and uncle.

According to her son, Mrs. Lindbergh was a skilled baker, who made pies, breads, and cakes in this Majestic woodstove. A woodbox is set behind the table.

The Home of
Andrew Jackson
1767–1845

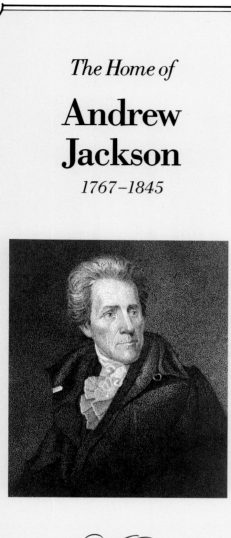

I for one do not despair of the republic; I have great confidence in the virtue of the great majority of the people, and I cannot fear the result.

From his letter to James Hamilton, Jr., June 29, 1828

A VISIT to Andrew Jackson's Tennessee estate, The Hermitage, provides a good introduction to the man who is remembered in American history as both a rugged frontiersman and a savvy political and military leader.

In 1787, the 21-year-old Jackson, born to a farm family and educated in the law, left his native North Carolina on horseback for a prosecuting attorney's job in frontier Tennessee. There he took an interest in politics, winning election to the state constitutional convention, serving as one of the state's first members of Congress (1797/98) and later in the Senate. He then spent six years on the bench of the state's highest court. In 1802 he was elected major general of the Tennessee state militia.

Two years later, Jackson bought 425 acres of land just east of Nashville for $3400. For 17 years, he and his wife, Rachel, lived in log cabins and raised cotton and prize thoroughbreds. During this time, Jackson became known as "Old Hickory," the heroic general who defeated the British in the Battle of New Orleans in 1815. Before he retired from the army in 1821, Jackson commissioned a brick Federal-style home of eight rooms for his property. It was completed shortly before his second term in the Senate (1823).

Jackson became the Democratic Party's presidential candidate in 1824. He won the popular vote but failed to gain a majority in the Electoral College. The outcome of the election was decided by the House of Representatives, which selected John Quincy Adams. In 1828, Old Hickory was nominated again, and this time he won. This charismatic leader—the first populist President—used his tenure in the White House (he was reelected in 1832) to expand the powers of the executive branch and to hold together the fragile Union.

In 1831, while in the White House, Jackson commissioned extensive additions to his frontier estate. He added two first-floor wings —one for a dining room, pantry, and kitchen; the other for a library and office. The old first-floor dining room and bedroom became back-to-back parlors, and the old parlors became bedrooms. In addition, a columned porch was attached to the front of the house.

A fire in 1834 destroyed the entire second floor, and Jackson again remodeled, this time in the Greek Revival style. The gabled roof was redesigned, and the porch was replaced by a two-story high-columned portico, giving the building the look of an Athenian temple.

Jackson returned home from the White House in 1837 and lived at The Hermitage until his death in 1845. Since 1889, the estate has been preserved by the Ladies' Hermitage Association. In 1989, on the Association's 100th birthday, it began an extensive restoration program of the The Hermitage.

After a fire in 1834, Andrew Jackson turned his colonial home into an impressive mansion in the Greek Revival style.

William Jennings Bryan

1860–1925

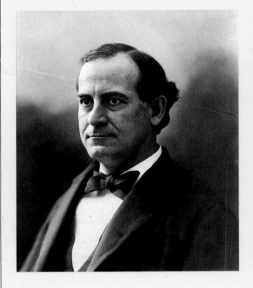

~

You shall not press down upon the brow of labor this crown of thorns. You shall not crucify mankind upon a cross of gold.

From his acceptance speech at the Democratic National Convention, 1896

Photograph. c. 1896. Library of Congress.

This handsome wooden stairway in the reception hall leads to the family bedrooms on the second floor. A portrait of Bryan greets Fairview's guests.

IN THE FALL of 1901, William Jennings Bryan, the great orator who had been twice defeated as a presidential candidate, began constructing a large home on his country estate three miles from downtown Lincoln, Nebraska. Bryan had been adding parcels of land to the estate, called "Fairview," since he bought the first five acres seven years before, envisioning a substantial home—the "Monticello of the West"—where statesmen and diplomats would stop on coast-to-coast trips.

The home, completed in 1903, in no way resembles or rivals Thomas Jefferson's creation in Charlottesville, Virginia (see pp. 92–94), but it is impressive, nonetheless. This Midwestern house, designed by Artemus A. Roberts, is an imposing Queen Anne Victorian of four stories, including a daylight basement and attic, with several gables and a large tower topped by a cone-shaped roof. The walls are brick, the roof is slate, and a columned porch (now enclosed) wraps around one corner of the house.

The basement was the living area for Bryan, his wife, Mary, and their three children. It contains the family dining room, a kitchen and pantry, a furnace and storage rooms, and a study where Bryan wrote speeches, books, and articles, including editorials for *The Commoner*, a newspaper which he had founded in 1901.

The main floor features a large central reception hall with a marble fireplace, a formal parlor, a curio room, and a library fanning out from the central hall, as well as a bedroom, a bathroom, and a small parlor in the rear. The rooms are filled with furnishings and mementos from Bryan's many overseas trips, and the walls hold portraits of some of the political leaders whom he admired.

The second floor contains four bedrooms and a schoolroom housed in the large front tower. A door in the schoolroom leads to the

Bryan's parlor was decorated with ornately carved furniture and elaborate Oriental carpets. Many of the art objects were collected during Bryan's overseas trips.

William Jennings Bryan hoped that this impressive Victorian home in Lincoln, Nebraska, would become the "Monticello of the West."

Bryan's daughters slept in this second-floor bedroom, which is restored with furnishings typical of the period.

second-floor porch, offering a splendid view of the surrounding countryside. The top floor holds small attic rooms.

In its heyday, Fairview comprised almost 350 acres. Bryan had been raised on a farm near Salem, Illinois, and he made sure that his children got a taste of farm life. He raised both crops and animals at Fairview, and much of the family's food was home grown. Near the house were gardens, shade trees, and a large lawn where Bryan hosted outdoor parties and held political rallies.

If Bryan's estate did not quite match Jefferson's, neither did his career, but he was one of America's leading politicians at the turn of the century. When his education was complete, he moved to Lincoln, Nebraska, to join a classmate's law firm and, in 1890, at age 30, he became the state's first Democratic congressman. In the House he became known as a dynamic orator, and his famous "Cross of Gold" speech at the 1896 Democratic National Convention paved the way for his first presidential nomination. All told, he lost three bids for the presidency, though he got some satisfaction from Woodrow Wilson's 1912 victory, since he had been instrumental in securing the New Jersey Governor's nomination. Moreover, he served as Wilson's Secretary of State for three years (1913–1915).

Politically, Bryan is often considered a conservative, perhaps because most Americans know him as the man who successfully prosecuted John T. Scopes for teaching Darwinian evolution in the famous 1925 "monkey" trial in Dayton, Tennessee. But Bryan championed such "radical" causes as voting rights for women, the direct election of senators, and the establishment of a federal income tax.

When his political career ended in 1916, Bryan and his wife retired to Florida. He deeded his land in Lincoln to the Nebraska Methodist Conference as a hospital site, and Fairview became a dormitory for student nurses. He died in 1925 and is buried at Arlington National Cemetery.

In 1961, when the home was no longer in use, Bryan Memorial Hospital, the Nebraska State Historical Society, and the Junior League of Lincoln combined to restore the home and open it to visitors. Today Fairview, located at 4900 Sumner Street, is administered by Bryan Memorial Hospital and the Nebraska State Historical Society.

The Home of
George Rogers Clark
1752–1818

For in part it has been the influence of our posts on the Illinoise and Ouabash that have saved the frontiers and in a great measure baffled the designes of the Enemy at Detroit.

From the *George Rogers Clark Papers*

Painting by Joseph Bush. 1816. Courtesy Locust Grove.

The Croghan–Clark home at Locust Grove is a fine Georgian-style mansion made of brick pressed at the estate.

ALTHOUGH LOCUST GROVE, in Jefferson County, Kentucky, is known as the last home of George Rogers Clark, the estate is actually the place where two great Revolutionary War families, the Clarks of Virginia and the Croghans of Philadelphia, crossed paths at the end of the 18th century. The bond between the two families was formed when Jonathan Clark and William Croghan were both taken prisoner by the British at the Battle of Charlestown and then became lifelong friends.

Jonathan's brother, George Rogers Clark, was the Revolutionary War general whose victories against the British in the Illinois and Indiana territories enabled the colonists to retain control of the frontier during the conflict. After the war, General Clark began to explore the Kentucky counties that were, at the time, part of Virginia and took William Croghan, his

brother's friend, as a surveying partner. Croghan soon established a successful shipping business on the Ohio and Mississippi Rivers, and General Clark convinced the rest of his family to leave Virginia for the new territory. Croghan married Clark's sister, Lucy, in 1789, and soon afterward purchased 387 acres for an estate. He built a cabin on the land for himself and his new bride and began construction of a permanent house, which was completed in 1791.

The home is a 2½-story Georgian structure, made of brick pressed on the grounds, with double chimneys on each side of the gabled roof. A covered porch stretches across the back, providing a view of the estate's gardens and meadows.

The front door opens into a central hall-way running the width of the house. Furnished with benches, chairs, and end tables, the hall served as both a sitting room and an indoor breezeway during the long Kentucky summers. To the right of the front door are two dining rooms, one for informal family suppers and one for formal dinners. The family dining room has a door leading to a kitchen which is separate from the house. To the left of the front door are the front parlor and a rear bedroom, used by George Rogers Clark when he visited and later lived at the estate.

The second floor contains four rooms—the Croghans' bedroom, a guest room, a large ballroom used for receptions, and a retiring room adjacent to the ballroom. The small bedrooms on the third floor were used by the Croghans' nine children.

During the early years of the 19th century, Locust Grove played host to some of America's most important figures. In 1806, Vice President Aaron Burr visited George Rogers Clark at the estate. Later that year, Capt. Meriwether Lewis and Capt. William Clark, the general's younger brother, stayed at Locust Grove when they returned from their historic exploration of the vast territory of the Louisiana Purchase. John James Audubon, the painter and ornithologist, was a frequent visitor, and in 1819 the Croghans were hosts to former President James Monroe and Maj. Gen. Andrew Jackson.

In 1809, when his days as an Indian fighter and explorer had ended, George Rogers Clark, a lifelong bachelor, moved permanently to Locust Grove and spent the final decade of his life enjoying his nieces and nephews and hunting in the nearby woods. He died in 1818.

The Croghans owned Locust Grove until 1878, when it was sold to the James Paul family. Five years later, it was sold again to Richard Waters, and his descendants held title to it until 1961, when the Commonwealth of Kentucky and Jefferson County bought the house and 55 surrounding acres and began restoration. A wing built in 1837, Victorian trim, and plumbing were removed. Because the original furniture had disappeared, the house was furnished with period pieces collected from the surrounding area. In 1964, Locust Grove was opened to visitors. Today, the estate is owned by Jefferson County and administered by the Historic Homes Foundation.

(Opposite) Filled with benches, chairs, and end tables, the wide first-floor hallway, running the width of the house, served as a breezeway and sitting room.

Since few original Locust Grove furnishings are still in existence, those displayed are authentic to the period in which George Rogers Clark was in residence. The room pictured here is the first-floor parlor.

During the last three months of his life, Jesse James lived in this single-story house in St. Joseph, Missouri.

The Home of

Jesse James

1847–1882

I have written many letters vindicating myself of the false charges that have been brought against me. Detectives have been trying for years to get positive proof against me for some criminal offense, so that they could get a large reward offered for me, dead or alive.

From his letter to *The Kansas City Times,* August 18, 1876

Photograph. c. 1875. Library of Congress.

J ESSE JAMES spent his boyhood years on his family's farm in western Missouri. As teenagers, he and his brother Frank left home to ride with Quantrill's Raiders, an "irregular" (guerrilla) force led by Confederate Gen. William Quantrill, that forayed into Kansas and Missouri during the Civil War. Though the James brothers returned for a time to the farm after the war, they soon resumed their forays and became known as outlaws and highwaymen who roamed the rugged Kansas–Missouri border.

The first big robbery to which their names were attached occurred in Liberty, Missouri, on February 13, 1866. A dozen bandits under the direction of the James brothers robbed a bank in broad daylight, the first time such a crime had been committed in the United States during peacetime. Within a few years, the James gang had progressed to train robberies, once loosening a rail on a blind curve to halt a train just outside of Council Bluffs, Iowa. Their names were also attached to robberies and murders in Texas, Montana, Arkansas, and Colorado.

Many thought that the only fitting home for Jesse James was a jail cell—to be occupied while he waited for a gallows to be built and

a hangman to arrive in town. But to others he was a hero, a modern-day Robin Hood who robbed from the rich and powerful and lived a life of high adventure. James himself claimed to be a law-abiding citizen. He married, fathered and supported two children, and constantly wrote letters to local newspapers denying involvement in the crimes that reporters credited to him. Although often accused, he was never convicted of anything.

Since the James family was frequently on the move, it is hardly surprising that Jesse's last home was a rented house, one in which he lived for only a little more than three months. On Christmas Eve in 1881, he, his wife, and their two children—living under the name of Howard—moved into the single-floor dwelling with the gabled roof on 1318 Lafayette Street, St. Joseph, Missouri, and paid the city councilman who owned the home a rent of $14 per month. Jesse liked the place because it was on top of a high hill; he could spot unwanted visitors easily from the front windows. There was good reason for Jesse's concern: Governor T. T. Crittenden had put a bounty of $10,000 on his head, a reward for his capture, dead or alive.

In the Jameses' day, the house had five rooms—a living room, dining room, two bedrooms, and a rear summer kitchen. On the morning of April 3, 1882, just after he had eaten breakfast, Jesse mounted a living room chair to straighten a picture hanging on the wall. With no warning, while his back was turned, Bob Ford, a member of his gang who was visiting the house, shot him in the back of the head. The bullet ripped through Jesse's skull and stuck into the living room wall; its victim fell to the floor dead.

Ford and his brother Charles were convicted of Jesse's murder, an illogical act perhaps given the dead-or-alive bounty on Jesse's head but an indication of the frontier's somewhat idiosyncratic legal system. At any rate, they were saved from hanging by the Governor's pardon. Charles committed suicide shortly thereafter, and Bob was later shot to death in a bar in Creede, Colorado. Frank James lived for another 30 years, never serving time in jail. Jesse's son, Jesse, Jr., became a lawyer, and his daughter moved to California, married, and raised a family.

Within days of Jesse's death, his last home became a tourist attraction, as citizens paraded through its rooms to see the bullet hole in the wall and the place where the outlaw had fallen. In the ensuing decades, the house's many occupants took full advantage of its notoriety, charging visitors a small fee for an inspection of the premises.

In 1939, the house on Lafayette Street was moved to the Belt Highway to attract tourists. In 1977, it was purchased by Robert Keatley and given to the Pony Express Historical Association. The house was moved again, to its present location in St. Joseph on the corner of 12th and Penn Streets, near the Patee House, the hotel where Mrs. James and her children stayed after Jesse's murder. Today, the Pony Express Historical Association maintains both the Jesse James Home and the Patee House Museum.

(Below left) A photograph of Jesse James hangs above the bed in his bedroom.

This organ, set in the living room, is a period piece, donated to the home. James was not musically inclined.

Abraham Lincoln

1809–1865

I would save the Union. I would save it the shortest way under the Constitution. The sooner the national authority can be restored; the nearer the Union will be "the Union as it was."

From his letter to Horace Greeley, August 22, 1862

Photograph by Alexander Gardiner. 1863. Library of Congress.

T HE POPULAR image of Abraham Lincoln is that of a frontiersman, a strapping man who cleared the land with an ax, lived in a log cabin, and bagged his food with a rifle. That image is, to some extent, accurate. He was born in a one-room cabin with a dirt floor in Sinking Spring, Kentucky, to frontier parents who were barely literate, although his father was a skilled carpenter as well as a farmer. When Abe was seven, the family moved to Indiana. As a young man Lincoln worked as a farmhand and rail splitter. Along the way, he gained an education, more on his own initiative than from frontier schoolmasters. He later clerked in a store and became village postmaster in New Salem, Illinois, near Springfield. Lincoln answered a call for volunteers during the Black Hawk War of 1832 and was unanimously elected captain by the New Salem troop. That same year, he ran as a Whig for the state legislature. He was defeated, but won a seat two years later and began his remarkable political career.

While serving in the Illinois State House, he studied law, gaining admission to the bar in 1836. After four terms in the legislature, he married Mary Todd, and the couple settled in Springfield, where Lincoln set up a law practice. For two years, they boarded at the Globe Tavern, but in 1844 they bought their own home, a three-year-old house on 8th and Jackson Streets owned by the minister who had married them two years earlier.

The house—the only one Lincoln owned—is the home of a successful lawyer, not a rugged frontiersman. When the Lincolns moved in, it was only 1½ stories tall with a small lot, but as the family grew—Edward was born in 1846, William in 1850, and Thomas in 1853—so did the house. By the mid-1850s, the Lincolns owned a stylish two-story, 10-room Victorian with a back porch and a brick wall surrounding the property. A carriage house and woodshed stood out back.

The first floor contains the family living area—front and rear parlors, a small sitting room, a kitchen where Mrs. Lincoln prepared scrumptious meals, and a dining room. Visitors claimed that the furnishings were "made for use and not for show," but the for-

In 1844 Abraham Lincoln purchased this two-story Victorian home in Springfield, Illinois; it was the only home he would ever own.

Since the first floor of the Lincolns' home contained no closets, the hall was equipped with a rack for hats and wraps. Pictured is a top hat, Lincoln's favorite type of headgear.

mal front parlor has a number of fashionable rococo pieces.

Upstairs are five bedrooms—four for the Lincolns and one for the family's live-in maid. Lincoln often worked at home, writing and polishing the speeches that would make him an important national figure in the newly formed Republican Party.

But Lincoln's early political career was marked more by defeat than by victory. As a Whig he won a seat in the House of Representatives in 1846, but he lost his bid for reelection due to his opposition to the Mexican War, which was favored by his expansionist-minded constituents. In 1858, as a candidate of the new Republican Party, he ran for the Senate against the Democratic incumbent, Stephen A. Douglas, and the two engaged in a series of memorable and nationally reported debates on slavery and other issues. Lincoln won great renown as an orator but again lost the election. In May 1860, however, a delegation of important Republicans came to the Springfield home to inform Lincoln that he had been nominated by the party to run for President. This time he defeated Douglas, the candidate of the Northern Democrats, as well as Vice President John C. Breckinridge, the candi-

This guest bedroom is simply furnished. A small woodstove is set in what was once a fireplace.

date of the Southern Democrats, and John Bell, the candidate of the Constitutional Union Party.

When Lincoln left for Washington on February 7, 1861, he thanked the people of Springfield for their help and good wishes. Saying that he owed everything to them, he left "not knowing when, or whether ever, I may return."

He did not return alive. After four years of civil war, a brutal conflict that nearly destroyed the country and aged him well beyond his years, Lincoln was murdered by John Wilkes Booth, a rabid supporter of the Southern cause, in Ford's Theater, just five days after Gen. Robert E. Lee had surrendered and peace seemed at hand. The President died on Good Friday, April 14, 1865; his body was sent by train to Springfield for burial.

After the President's death, the house in Springfield was rented to a series of tenants. One boarder, Osborn H. Oldroyd, asked Robert Todd Lincoln, the family's eldest son, to donate the house to the State of Illinois. He did so in 1887. Since then, the house and some of the furnishings have been restored, offering visitors an opportunity to see how Abraham Lincoln lived before he became President.

The Lincolns used functional furniture throughout the house, but the parlor, pictured here, contains a number of fashionable rococo pieces. A cast-iron woodstove was set in the fireplace for efficient heating.

Lincoln's bedroom doubled as a workroom; in it the future President wrote many of his stirring campaign speeches.

The Home of
Henry Ford
1863–1947

A man can never leave his business. He ought to think of it by day and dream of it by night.

THE HENRY FORD story is one of those rags-to-riches tales that can be used to extol the virtues of patience, hard work, and risk taking. Born in tiny Greenfield Township (now Dearborn), Michigan, in 1863, Ford left the security of the family farm at age 17 to pursue his interest in mechanics. He landed a job near Detroit with the Michigan Car Company, and he repaired watches and clocks for extra money. He later worked for Westinghouse and, in 1890, became chief engineer at the Edison Illuminating Company. During his spare time he tinkered with motors, and in 1893 he built his first gasoline engine.

Three years later, working essentially on his own, he designed and assembled his first automobile, a light carriage propelled by a two-cylinder engine. In 1899, he resigned from the Edison company and formed the Detroit Automobile Company.

Ford's new enterprise failed, but in 1903, with several assistants, he formed the Ford Motor Company. By using the newest assembly-line methods of production and by correctly judging that middle-class Americans were ready to buy cars, the Ford Motor Company achieved rapid success. Late in 1908, the company produced its first Model T, a reliable

In 1914, Henry Ford commissioned Fair Lane, this 56-room Scottish Baronial mansion on his estate in Dearborn, Michigan. The home is built entirely of concrete and Marblehead limestone.

The Fords' bedroom is the only room in the home with original furniture: Louis XVI mahogany beds and pieces of English Sheraton.

$825 automobile that average working Americans could afford. It changed the country and made Ford a multi-millionaire.

But Ford paid a price for such quick success. He enjoyed little privacy, and he had no opportunity to settle down. From the time of his marriage in 1888 through 1914, when the Ford Motor Company controlled almost 50% of the American car market, Henry and his wife, Clara, lived in 14 different homes. Both natives of Greenfield Township, they longed for a permanent and peaceful place where they could raise their son, Edsel, and enjoy the rewards of Henry's success.

In 1914, Ford commissioned construction of a large home on his 2000-acre property in Dearborn. Clara and Edsel took up residence in December 1915, and Henry moved in a month later, after an unsuccessful peace-seeking trip to Europe during World War I. Ford called his 56-room English modified mansion "Fair Lane," after the road in County Cork, Ireland, where Ford's maternal grandfather was born. (Years later, the Ford Motor Company would use the name, spelled as one word, for one of its most successful models.)

With its turrets and parapets, the two-story concrete and limestone building resembles, on one side, a medieval castle; on the other, the low, horizontal lines of the Prairie school of architecture. Gardens, meadows, waterscapes, and terraces surround the house, once requiring a grounds-keeping staff of 25 people. A powerhouse, connected to the mansion by a tunnel, shelters a 12-car garage, a laboratory, and three generators designed to make Fair Lane self-sufficient.

The main-floor entrance hall leads to a living room with French walnut paneling, antique brass fixtures, and a marble fireplace. At the rear of the living room is the Fords' favorite spot, the sun porch, which they used as an informal parlor. (Another special place is the rustic field room located in the basement, where the Fords enjoyed dancing.) The other first-floor rooms are the formal dining room, a kitchen and pantry, a billiard room, a library, a music room, and a swimming pool (now a restaurant).

The second floor, reached by a spectacular oak staircase, contains two suites — one for Henry and Clara, the other for Edsel — and the Thomas Edison Room, where the great inventor, once a neighbor of Ford, slept when he visited. Also included on this floor are extra rooms for servants and guests.

This home was indeed a permanent one. The Fords lived in it until their deaths — Henry in 1947, Clara in 1950. During the last years of his life, Henry saw great expansion and innovation, as well as increased competition, in the automobile industry. He endowed a number of charities, including the Ford Foundation, which funds scientific and educational projects.

After Clara Ford's death, Fair Lane became a home for the Ford Archives. In 1957, the Ford Motor Company donated the mansion and 210 acres of the estate to the University of Michigan for its Dearborn campus. The university continues to manage Fair Lane, using it as a cultural and educational center.

This oval-shaped sitting room with large, comfortable couches and stylish serving tables was used by the Fords for informal gatherings. The formal parlor was more elaborately decorated.

The downstairs field room, where the Fords took dance lessons, features an oak floor with walnut pegs, a field stone fireplace, and hand-carved wooden cornices. When the Fords entertained visitors, the table was typically set for cookies and tea.

Ford's oak-paneled library once held more than 4000 volumes, including many rare books and first editions. Authors represented included the Brownings, James Fenimore Cooper, Ralph Waldo Emerson, Henry David Thoreau, and Mark Twain.

William F. Cody

1846–1917

My great forte in killing buffaloes from horseback was to get them circling by riding my horse at the head of the herd, shooting the leaders, thus crowding their followers to the left till they would finally circle round and round.

From his autobiography, *The Life and Times of Buffalo Bill Cody*

In 1886, this 19-room Victorian with gingerbread trim was built on Buffalo Bill's 4000-acre ranch in Nebraska.

THE NAME "BUFFALO BILL" is synonymous with the Wild West. Along with "Doc" Holliday, "Wild Bill" Hickok, and Wyatt Earp, William Frederick Cody has gone down in American legend as one of the rough-and-tumble frontiersmen who helped tame the Old West. In this case, the legend has some basis in fact.

Bill Cody was born in 1846 in Scott County, Iowa—frontier country. When he was a child, his family pushed even further west, moving to Salk Creek Valley, Kansas. At age 12, Bill signed on as a bullwhaker with the westbound Russell & Majors wagon train. Two years later, he became one of the Pony Express's youngest riders. During his teenage years, he also worked as a trapper and panned for gold during the Pike's Peak gold rush.

In 1864, the 18-year-old Cody joined the Union forces during the Civil War. Two years later, after the war's conclusion, he was hired as an army scout and guide, a role he continued to perform until 1873. During those years, he built a reputation as an Indian fighter and a horseman with few peers, one who could ride for days without sleep. He became "Buffalo Bill" in the late 1860s, when he was hired to provide buffalo meat for the men who worked on the Kansas Pacific Railroad. He is said to have officially claimed the name after winning a buffalo hunting contest near Sheridan, Kansas.

In the late 1870s, Cody capitalized on his reputation as an Indian fighter and buffalo hunter by acting in stage plays about the frontier and, later, by assembling and touring with the Wild West Exhibition, a sort of traveling rodeo and Wild West show, which he eventually brought to Chicago, the east coast, and Europe.

During the 1880s, when the Exhibition was making him a wealthy man, Buffalo Bill bought 4000 acres of land in North Platte, Nebraska, and established Scout's Rest Ranch. There he raised high-grade cattle and fine thoroughbred horses for sale. In 1886, Cody directed his brother-in-law and ranch manager, Al Goodman, to build a large home on the ranch suitable for Buffalo Bill, his wife, and their children.

We might expect that Buffalo Bill's home would be a low-lying prairie house with a long porch and a hitching post and water trough in front. But Goodman left the design of the house to his wife, and she enlisted architect Patrick Walsh to build a large Victorian of 18 rooms.

The two-story house with a large central tower, various gables, odd-shaped bays, and gingerbread trim seems better suited to a Gothic thriller than a western. But Buffalo Bill

Mrs. Cody's second-floor bedroom is tastefully furnished. The doors lead to the balcony above the front porch.

The caption for this portrait of Buffalo Bill and Sitting Bull reads, "Foes in '76, Friends in '85." A crank music box sits on the table under the painting.

liked the home and kept it filled with businessmen, politicians, promoters, actors, and any eastern dignitaries who dared to venture into the Wild West. The dwelling was comfortable and tastefully furnished—a symbol of high society on the Nebraska prairie.

The first floor holds a den where Cody conducted business transactions, a living room, a bedroom, a kitchen, a family dining room, and a rear dining hall where the ranch's hired hands ate their meals. Upstairs there are 10 bedrooms used by the Codys, their children, and the ranch's many visitors. Several of the bedrooms are odd-shaped, conforming to the gables and angles of the home. A second-floor stairway leads to the large central tower. The room here features windows on all sides and was used to spot visitors as they approached the ranch.

Cody owned Scout's Rest until 1911, when some bad business transactions forced him to sell it to Gordon W. Lillie ("Pawnee Bill"), one of his partners in the Wild West Exhibition, for $100,000. The Codys stayed on at the ranch until 1913, then moved to Cody, Wyoming, a town Buffalo Bill had founded 15 years earlier. He died at his sister's home in Denver in 1917, at age 70.

Scout's Rest Ranch passed through several owners after the Codys' departure, and it remained vacant for long periods. In 1961, the Kuhlmann family sold the ranch to the State of Nebraska, which opened it as a state historical park in 1965. The home, the large barn, and the surviving outbuildings were carefully restored and opened for visitors. Today, the ranch is administered by the Nebraska Game and Parks Commission.

Buffalo Bill's stable, built in 1887, was
designed to accommodate 80 horses. Cody
raised thoroughbreds on the ranch for sale.

The Home of
Harry S Truman
1884–1972

I tried never to forget who I was and where I'd come from and where I was going back to.

From *Plain Speaking: An Oral Biography of Harry S Truman* by Merle Miller

Photograph. c. 1945. U.S. Army. Courtesy Harry S Truman Library.

HARRY S TRUMAN, the 33rd President of the United States, spent most of his last 50 years in a pleasant Victorian home on 219 North Delaware Street, in Independence, Missouri.

Truman was born on a farm in Lamar, Missouri, in 1884, and moved to Independence when he was six years old. After high school — he could not afford college — he worked as a bookkeeper, bank clerk, and farmer, then entered the army and fought heroically in France during World War I. Upon his return to civilian life, he married Bess Wallace, his childhood sweetheart, and they moved into her grandparent's house on North Delaware Street.

The home is a 2½-story 14-room Victorian with gables and angles and splendid porches. Mrs. Truman's grandmother and mother shared the home with the Trumans and their daughter, Margaret, born in 1924.

The front porch leads to a large central hallway. Off the hall are a parlor/music room with an adjacent library and the family living room. Downstairs are a bedroom, and the dining room, flanked by a pantry and kitchen. On the second floor are several bedrooms, including the one used by Harry and Bess. The top floor is an attic.

In 1922, Truman launched his political career when a local Democratic Party boss convinced him to run for a county judgeship. He won, performed admirably, and used his popularity to win a U.S. Senate seat in 1934. In 1944, President Franklin D. Roosevelt chose him as running mate and he was elected Vice President. When Roosevelt died in April 1945, Truman became President. He led the United States through the final days of World War II, directed the Marshall Plan that helped rebuild war-torn Europe, and in 1948 won another term in one of the great election upsets, defeating Thomas E. Dewey, the Republican candidate favored by the pollsters.

In 1953, the Trumans left Washington and retired to Independence. They bought the home on North Delaware Street from Bess's mother's estate, immediately modernized the kitchen and added new carpeting and wallpaper. The first-floor library became Truman's refuge for reading and writing.

Harry Truman died in 1972, at the age of 88. Bess lived another 10 years. Upon her death, she bequeathed their home to the federal government. Today, the home is administered by the National Park Service. Visitors can also tour the Harry S Truman Library and Museum a few blocks away.

When Harry Truman married Bess Wallace in 1919, the couple moved into her parents' home on North Delaware Street in Independence, Missouri. The Secret Service added the iron fence for security when Truman became President.

The Home of

Frank Lloyd Wright

1867–1959

No house should ever be on any hill or on anything. It should be of the hill, belonging to it, so hill and house could live together each the happier for the other.

From *An Autobiography*

Photograph. c. 1950. Library of Congress.

Wright designed this barrel-shaped second-floor room as a playroom for his children.

(Opposite) A steel chain harness partially supports the balcony in the drafting room of Frank Lloyd Wright's studio.

IN HIS LATER years, architect Frank Lloyd Wright would look back with embarrassment on his home and studio at the corner of Forest and Chicago Avenues in Oak Park, Illinois, considering it the work of a crude beginner. Today, students of architecture study the home for two reasons: first, because it was only the second building totally designed by the man who ushered American architecture into the modern age; and, second, because it employs some of the techniques that Wright would develop to great effect later in his career.

Wright moved to the Chicago area in 1887, when he was 20 years old, seeking a job as an architect, a career he had wanted since he first played with building blocks and colored paper — "gifts" designed by the German educator Friedrich Froebel and supplied by his mother. Wright worked first for a family friend, then joined the firm of Adler and Sullivan. In 1889, he married Catherine Tobin, bought a piece of land in Oak Park—near the residence of friends with whom he was living — and designed his first home.

The house on Forest Avenue was ready for occupancy before the Wrights' first child was born in 1890. Like many other Oak Park homes built after the Civil War, Wright's two-story shingled cottage was fronted by a large Queen Anne gable and surrounded by a terrace. But Wright, never an imitator, deviated from traditional models. In contrast to the high gable, for example, the eaves are low and broad, making the home look as though it were built close to the ground, a feature which set it apart from Oak Park's rambling Victorian dwellings.

Wright's new abode originally had three downstairs rooms and two upstairs bedrooms and a studio, but by 1895 the couple had four children, and Wright saw the need for expansion. He attached an addition to the rear of the house to hold a new kitchen and an upstairs playroom with a unique barrel-shaped ceiling for the children. He divided his upstairs studio into bedrooms and soon afterward began to build a new studio adjacent to the house.

Connected to the home by an entrance hall, the studio, completed in 1897, comprises four rooms—an octagonal library, a two-story polygonal drafting room with a balcony sup-

YE'VE LEFT A GLIMMER STILL TO CHEER
THE MAN—THE ARTIFEX
THAT HOLDS IN SPITE O'KNOCKS AND SCALE
O'FRICTION WASTE AN' SLIP,
AN' BY THAT LIGHT—NOW MARK MY WORD—
WE'LL BUILD THE PERFECT SHIP.

ported by thick steel chains, an office for Wright with a bedroom above, and a reception room. The studio employs some of the innovations that would mark Wright as a 20th-century architectural genius: assymmetrical rooms with varying levels between them; hidden entranceways that break down the barrier between a building and its immediate surroundings; minimal partitions between rooms to suggest openness; and a low, flat roof that gives the building a horizontal rather than vertical composition.

While working in this studio, Wright completed some of his most impressive projects — the Robie House in Chicago, the Larkin Office Building in Buffalo, and the Unity Temple in Oak Park. During this time, Wright and his associates also developed what became known as the Prairie school of architecture — long, horizontal structures which blend into the Midwestern and Western landscape, a uniquely American approach that flatly contradicted the French Beaux Arts style that had become fashionable in the late 19th century.

In 1909, Wright left his wife and moved to Europe. When he returned to the United States two years later he set up new living and working quarters in Spring Garden, Wisconsin. However, he supervised extensive renovations to the Oak Park home, essentially converting it into an apartment house. In 1923, he moved to California and, a few years later, sold the Oak Park property. During the next 30 years, he created numerous homes, office buildings, skyscrapers, and churches. One of his later masterworks is the Guggenheim Museum in New York City. His last house/studio was "Taliesin West," near Phoenix, Arizona. He died in 1959, at age 92, having designed more than 430 buildings.

In 1975, the Frank Lloyd Wright Home and Studio Foundation began the task of restoring the Oak Park estate to its condition in 1911, when Wright last lived and worked there. The project was completed in 1987. Today, the foundation offers tours of the property and administers its restoration and education programs.

(Opposite) **This stairway in the drafting room leads to the overhanging balcony.**

Wright's home in Oak Park, Illinois, is fronted by a Queen Anne gable and surrounded by a terrace; the studio, on the left, was added in 1897.

The Home of
Ulysses S. Grant
1822–1885

No terms except an unconditional and immediate surrender can be accepted. I propose to move immediately upon your works.

From his statement to the Confederate commander, Ft. Donelson, February 16, 1862

Photograph by William Barner of the James Studio. 1879. Illinois Historic Preservation Agency. Galena, IL.

I N AN ESSAY comparing Ulysses S. Grant and Robert E. Lee, Bruce Catton, the Civil War historian, states that the two great generals "were in complete contrast, representing two diametrically opposed elements in American life." Grant was the emergent modern man, representing "the great age of steel and machinery, of crowded cities and a restless burgeoning vitality." Lee, on the other hand, represented "the age of chivalry transplanted to a New World" and "embodied a way of life that had come down through the age of knighthood and the English country squire."

Nowhere is this contrast more obvious than in the locales that each man called home. Before the Civil War, Lee lived at stately Arlington House (see pp. 112–113), his wife's family's 1100-acre plantation in old Virginia. Grant, on the other hand, lived in Galena, a northwestern Illinois town that had boomed in the 1820s to 1840s as a lead mining center and river port.

Grant, born and raised in Ohio and educated at the U.S. Military Academy, came to Galena in 1860 to work with his two brothers in his father's leather goods store for $50 a month. He, his wife, Julia, and their four young children lived on High Street on a hill overlooking downtown. In 1861, after the first skirmishes of the Civil War, Grant, who had served as an officer in the Mexican War, began to train a group of local volunteers. Soon afterward, he received a commission as colonel in command of the 21st Regiment of Illinois Infantry.

Grant distinguished himself in early campaigns and quickly reached the rank of major general. His significant victories at Ft. Donelson and Vicksburg ultimately led to his appointment as commander in chief of the Union armies. In April 1865, after many hard-fought battles, Grant received General Lee's surrender at Appomattox Courthouse in Virginia, virtually ending the war.

On August 18, 1865, Grant returned to Galena a national hero. Parades and ceremonies honored the man who had subdued the South. Moreover, a group of local Republicans led by congressman Elihu B. Washburne purchased a five-year-old furnished house on Bouthillier Street as a suitable reward for their hero. Although the Grants spent only short periods of time per year in Galena, they became fond of their home and used it as a stopping-off place on their many journeys.

The Italianate two-story brick house, designed by William Dennison, consists of two rectilinear blocks, with overhanging eaves, fronted by a columned porch topped by a

An engraving of Abraham Lincoln hangs above the fireplace in Grant's library. The marble sculpture on the small table is by popular sculptor John Rogers. It shows Grant, Lincoln, and Secretary of War Edwin M. Stanton planning battle strategy during the Civil War.

When the Civil War ended, a group of Galena, Illinois, citizens bought Ulysses S. Grant this Italianate brick home.

balustrade. The first floor holds a parlor, a library where Grant read and wrote, a dining room, and a kitchen housed in a small wing. Upstairs are bedrooms used by the Grants and their children.

In 1868, Grant easily won election as President. He was a popular Chief Executive, but his administration was marred by scandal. After two terms in the White House, Grant and his wife took a two-year trip around the world. They returned to Galena in 1879 for another welcome home celebration. They left again but returned in 1880. Then they moved to New York City. Grant died at Mt. McGregor, New York, in 1885.

In 1904, the Grants' children donated the house to the City of Galena as a memorial to their father. In 1931, it was given to the State of Illinois, which undertook extensive restoration of the home in 1955. Today, it is managed by the Illinois Historic Preservation Agency.

The dining room at the Grants' home is set for a formal dinner; the dishes, made for the Grants' daughter's wedding, were used while the family lived at the White House.

Daniel Boone

1734–1820

I returned home to my family with determination to bring them as soon as possible, at the risk of my life and fortune, to live in Kentucky, which I esteemed a second paradise.

From his *Autobiography*

Engraving by J. B. Longacre from a painting by Chester Harding. 1820. Library of Congress.

MOST AMERICANS know Daniel Boone as an explorer, a restless wanderer who journeyed on foot, by horseback, and by canoe into the American wilderness, clearing the land and establishing settlements, then moving further west into uncharted territory. Surely, many of his exploits have been embellished by storybooks and television shows. Nonetheless, Boone's reputation as an explorer and woodsman is certainly well deserved.

He was born near Reading, Pennsylvania, in 1734, the son of a Quaker farmer. Though he had little formal schooling, he learned to read and write, and he mastered mathematics well enough to earn a living as a surveyor. When Daniel was 16 years old the family moved to Virginia, and two years later he purchased land in northwestern North Carolina. He married Rebecca Bryan there.

He had heard tales of Kentucky's beauty and rich farmland, and he set off with his brother Squire and five men to explore that unmarked wilderness. Impressed with what he saw, he returned home in 1771 where his tales convinced a score of North Carolinians to head west to establish a settlement in Kentucky. Skirmishes with the Shawnees made many of them turn back, but Boone stayed and eventually founded a settlement, Boonesborough, on the Kentucky River in 1775. He made peace with the Shawnees, helped defend his settlement against the British during the Revolutionary War, and later served as a militia officer and legislator for the Kentucky territories.

After 10 years in Kentucky, Boone was on the move again, first north to Point Pleasant on the Ohio River, then, in 1797, further west into Missouri Territory, where he was empowered

(Opposite) In 1803, when he was almost 70 years old, Daniel Boone and his son, Nathan, began construction on this large Georgian-style home with walls of thick blue limestone.

Daniel's bedroom, near the north entrance of the house, is furnished as it was on the day Boone died.

(Opposite) This two-seated chair is set in
the drawing room. Throughout the house,
plain plaster walls are accented with black
walnut beams and trim.

A large stone fireplace occupies most of
one wall in the family dining room.

The decorations here are simple, befitting
the home of a frontiersman: a colored jug
is set in a drawing room window.

with civil and military authority under the Spanish government. He acquired land after the Louisiana Purchase of 1803 and, when he was more than 60 years old, he finally decided to settle down.

He chose a site in eastern Missouri, about 35 miles from St. Louis. There, in 1803, he and his son, Nathan, began to create a permanent home in the Georgian style for their families.

The house is built of Missouri blue limestone and is as strong and solid as the man who built it. A wide two-story gallery extends across the entire southern front, providing a splendid view of the surrounding countryside. The first floor is entered by a staircase within

the house and from the south front. It serves as the main dining room and kitchen. The door on the north front of the house leads to the main floor, which features a drawing room with a large fireplace, Daniel and Rebecca's private bedchamber, and a dining room. The third floor bedchambers were used by Nathan and his wife and family. The fourth floor is the ballroom for entertaining guests.

Throughout the house the plain plaster walls are accented with rich black walnut woodwork and beam ceilings. It was written at the time that the Boone Mansion was the finest home west of the Mississippi. Today it is restored to its early 19th-century condition.

Rebecca Boone died only a few years

after this wilderness home was completed, but Daniel lived to the age of 86. He died on September 26, 1820, in the bedchamber at the north front of the house. Both husband and wife were buried in Missouri, but years later, in 1845, remains thought to be theirs were moved to Frankfort, Kentucky. Today it is widely believed that Daniel and Rebecca still lie in Missouri soil.

The settlement of pioneers that grew up around the Boones will be the focus of Boonesfield Village which is being created near the Daniel Boone Home. Here, residing craftsmen will demonstrate the daily activities of settlers who lived in the area more than 150 years ago.

The Home of
Benjamin Harrison
1833–1901

*Great lives never go out. They
go on.*

From his address at Mt. McGregor,
New York, site of President Grant's death

Photograph. c. 1888-93. Library of
Congress.

The dining room in the
Harrison home is set for
a holiday dinner party.
The Harrisons had a
reputation for splendid
formal dinners.

IN 1874, Gen. Benjamin Harrison, Civil
War hero, engaged H.T. Brandt to build a
house on a double lot on North Delaware
Street in Indianapolis, not far from Harrison's
downtown law office.

Brandt designed a 16-room Italianate brick
home suitable for a successful lawyer, his wife,
and their two teenage children. The Italianate
style, which imitates early-Renaissance architecture, became popular in the United States in
the mid-19th century because it could be used
for both public buildings and private homes, in
rural or urban settings, and because it could
appear stately without looking pretentious.

Like other Italianate buildings, Harrison's
three-story brick home is irregular in shape
with a low-pitched roof, overhanging eaves, and
narrow single windows. A columned porch
stretches across the front of the house and
partially across one side.

The door on the front porch leads to an
entry hall to which all the other first-floor rooms
are attached. On the left are back-to-back
parlors and Harrison's library, which houses
his large collection of books. On the right is
an imposing, tastefully furnished dining room,
and in the rear are the kitchen and pantry,
which were added in the 1890s when Harrison made renovations.

The second floor holds the bedrooms. The
master suite includes a bedchamber, a large
sitting room, and a small dressing room. Across
the hall are two smaller rooms, probably used
by the Harrison children, and down the hall is
a large guest suite. The servants' quarters also
occupy the second floor, though they are kept
separate from the family bedrooms by an interior dividing wall. A narrow staircase leads from
the servants' quarters to the kitchen below.

It was a perfect house for a successful lawyer, but Harrison's political activities soon took
him elsewhere. Riding his Civil War popularity,
he was elected to the U.S. Senate from Indiana,
serving from 1881 to 1887. In 1888 he became

the Republican Party's presidential nominee, and defeated the incumbent, Grover Cleveland, in the general election by a small margin. Thus, Harrison continued his family's tradition of public service: his great-grandfather, Benjamin Harrison, was a signer of the Declaration of Independence, and a three-term Governor of Virginia; his grandfather, Gen. William Henry Harrison, was a hero of the War of 1812, a Senator from Ohio and the ninth President of the United States; and his father, John Scott Harrison, was an Ohio congressman.

Defeated in 1892 by Cleveland in his bid for reelection, Harrison returned to Indianapolis to resume his law practice. His wife, Caroline, had died in Washington in 1891, but in 1896 he married her niece, Mary Scott Lord, and the couple lived in the home on North Delaware Street until his death in 1901.

After her husband's death, Mrs. Harrison moved to New York and rented out the Indianapolis home. In 1937, she sold it to the Arthur Jordan Foundation, which used it as a dormitory for students of the Jordan School of Music. In 1973, the home was closed for complete restoration, and it was opened a year later as a memorial to the 23rd President of the United States.

A handsome bookcase, built especially for the room, occupies one wall in Harrison's library.

In 1874, Benjamin Harrison built this Italianate brick home near his law office in Indianapolis.

The Home of
Molly Brown
1867–1926

It simply can't go down, because I'm on it and I'm unsinkable.

On the sinking of the *Titanic*, according to her obituary in *The New York Times*, October 28, 1938.

THE MEMBERS of Denver's "Sacred 36" who scorned Molly Brown and her husband when they moved to town in 1894 might be surprised to hear that today her home on Pennsylvania Avenue is a monument. The Molly Brown House Museum stands as a tribute to the feisty woman who battled Denver's high society and eventually earned its respect.

Molly—born Margaret Tobin—hailed from Hannibal, Missouri, Mark Twain's hometown. At age 18, she left home to live with her half sister and brother-in-law, who were mining in Leadville, Colorado. There Molly met James Joseph Brown, a Pennsylvanian who had also come to Colorado to search for mineral wealth. Molly and James married, made a fortune in gold, and moved to Denver.

The home that the Browns purchased for $30,000 was a sprawling Victorian structure solidly built with cut Colorado lava-stone. It had been designed by William Lang, a Denver architect, in 1889. Like most Victorian homes, it is asymmetrical, a handsome conglomeration of gables, bays, porches, and balconies with large chimneys poking through the roof. The house is surrounded by a lava-stone porch and retaining wall, erected by the Browns after they moved in.

The three-story dwelling provided comfortable living quarters for James and Molly, their two children, and several servants. The first floor contains an attractive entry hall with a Turkish corner, a formal front parlor for entertaining, a rear parlor for the family, a library, a large dining room, and a kitchen. The second floor has five bedrooms and a sun-room leading to a balcony. Servants lived on the top floor and above the lava-stone and brick carriage house in the yard.

Despite their fine home, their active participation in civic organizations, and their fondness for socializing, the Browns were not accepted into Denver's high society. The Sacred 36 who directed the city's important social events resented the newcomers with their poor Irish background. Molly joined the Women's Club and James the Athletic Club, but the Browns were never offered an invitation by the old guard.

But that changed in 1912 when Molly survived the destruction of the "unsinkable" *Titanic.* She was forced into a lifeboat after helping dozens of women and children leave the sinking ship, and she took charge of the survivors, even raising money for their relief when they were safely ashore. She returned to

(Previous pages) **A shelf in the kitchen of Kit Carson's home in Taos, New Mexico, holds pottery, baskets, and other utensils made by local craftsmen.** (see pp. 164-167)

The entrance hall features an attractive Turkish corner; the oak stairway leads to the second-floor bedrooms.

In 1894, the Browns purchased this handsome five-year-old Victorian home built with cut Colorado lava-stone.

Denver an international heroine — and shortly afterward received a party invitation from Mrs. Crawford Hill, a leading member of the Sacred 36.

Molly Brown also became Denver's first preservationist, buying the home of Eugene Field, a local poet and journalist, and giving it to the city as a memorial in 1930. Two years later, Molly died while staying at the Barbizon Hotel in New York.

After Molly's death, her home passed through the hands of several owners. In 1971, it was rescued from demolition and restored by Historic Denver, Inc., a nonprofit organization dedicated to preserving the city's historical and architectural heritage. Molly's life has been immortalized by the popular musical, *The Unsinkable Molly Brown.*

This late-19th-century silk-shaded lamp sits on a table in the second-floor sun-room.

The first-floor library contains a piano and floor-to-ceiling bookcases. Molly, who lacked a formal education, was often tutored in this room.

The Browns' servants ate their meals in the kitchen. Food was prepared in the coal- and wood-burning stove.

Will Rogers was born in this handsome two-story home on his family's cattle ranch near Claremore, Oklahoma, in 1879.

FIFTY YEARS AFTER his death, Will Rogers is still remembered for his "down home" humor and homespun country wisdom. The cowboy humorist who delighted at gently ribbing the high and mighty began by working on his father's ranch and mingling with the local cowhands.

Rogers was born in 1879 on his family's ranch house on the Verdigris River near Oologah, in the Oklahoma Indian Territory. He claimed that his mother, Mary, was preparing for the birth in the rear frame section of their four-year-old two-story home, but just before delivery she moved to a front bedroom in the log part of the house because she had just read a biography of Abe Lincoln. "So I got the log house end of it okay," Rogers said. "All I need now is the other qualifications."

The home of Mary and Clem Rogers is unpretentious and functional, designed to meet the simple needs and tastes of a cattle-raising family. The front door, covered by a two-story gabled porch, leads to a small foyer and a central hallway that connects five rooms. The bedroom where Will was born is on the right, in front of the house, opposite the living room. At the rear is another bedroom, a dining room, and a kitchen. A staircase in the dining room leads to two upstairs bedrooms. Brick chimneys on either side of the house accommodate four open fireplaces which warmed the family during Oklahoma winters.

As a boy, Rogers learned to rope and ride, but at age 19 he left the family ranch to travel, including a stint in South America working with a Wild West show. Enthralled with show business, he joined the New York vaudeville circuit and developed the practice of making dryly humorous comments about current events and politicans between fancy lariat tricks. Soon the witty Oklahoman was famous — a *Ziegfeld Follies* performer, a syndicated newspaper columnist, and, in the 1930s, a radio and movie star. People around the country knew Rogers as the author of sayings like "All I know is what I read in the papers."

Though his theatrical career took him all over the country, Rogers kept close tabs on the family ranch. After his parents' deaths, he bought the ranch from his sisters, hired his nephew to run it, and made plans for expansion. In 1935, however, he and the famous pilot Wiley Post died in a plane crash near Point Barrow, Alaska. Will left behind his wife, Betty, and three children. He was 55 years old.

In 1959, the Rogers family deeded the ranch to the State of Oklahoma. A year later, the house was moved a mile west in anticipation of the construction of the Oologah Dam and Reservoir. Today, the first-floor rooms are open to visitors, and the upstairs is undergoing restoration.

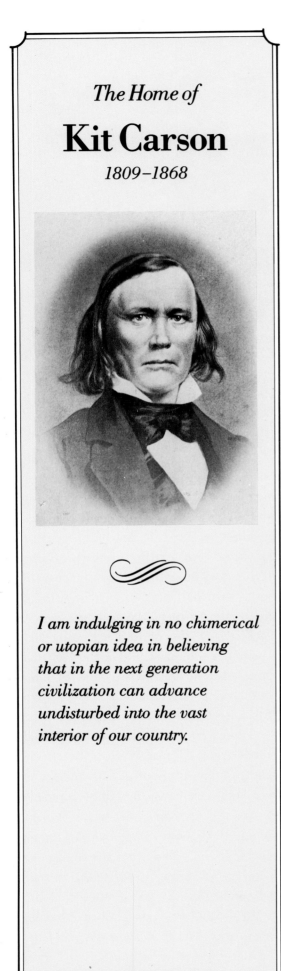

The Home of
Kit Carson
1809–1868

I am indulging in no chimerical or utopian idea in believing that in the next generation civilization can advance undisturbed into the vast interior of our country.

Photograph. c. 1845-60. Library of Congress.

THE HEROES on the Old West—men like Daniel Boone, "Buffalo Bill" Cody, and Kit Carson—rarely remained in one place very long. When settlements grew up around them, they moved on to uncharted territory, living in houses that were temporary shelters rather than homes.

Carson was born in a log cabin on the western Kentucky frontier in 1809. When he was a child, his family pressed westward to Missouri. At age 16, he signed on with a wagon train heading toward the Sante Fe Trail and New Mexico. The leader of the expedition was Charles Bent, who would later become New Mexico's first territorial governor.

In New Mexico, where he became known as an expert trapper and a fearless Indian fighter, Carson surprisingly set down roots. In 1842, his first wife, an Indian woman, died. A year later, he married Josefa Jaramillo, a member of one of Taos's oldest families and a sister-in-law of Charles Bent. As a wedding present for Josefa, Carson purchased a single-story 12-room adobe with a dirt floor near the town plaza in Taos. The 18-year-old U-shaped home was solidly built, with 30-inch-thick adobe walls and large wooden beams supporting the ceilings. The small windows had no panes but were covered with wooden shutters to keep out the daytime southwestern heat. The roof was made with wooden planks overlaid with about 2 feet of packed dirt. Most of the rooms had adobe fireplaces forged into one of the corners, a building practice that the early Spanish settlers of the Southwest had adopted from the Pueblo Indians who had originally settled the region.

When Carson moved in, he modernized the house substantially, installing wooden floors, glass window panes, and a sloping wooden roof over the packed earth that topped the house. He furnished the rooms tastefully with pieces transported from the Midwest via the Sante Fe Trail. The family living room was

In 1843, Kit Carson purchased this 12-room adobe as a wedding present to his new wife.

The Carsons' kitchen features a thick wood-block table and frontier utensils made by local craftsmen.

The kitchen fireplace, like the others in the home, is set in the corner of the room. Spanish settlers adapted this feature from the dwellings of Pueblo Indians.

decorated with Victorian chairs and end tables, furnishings that one might expect to see in a Chicago or New York drawing room rather than an adobe house in Taos. Carson's bedroom had a handsome wooden bed frame and upholstered easy chairs, yet his furnishings also included pieces common to the region. The kitchen, for example, had a thick wood-block table and cooking utensils made by local craftsmen. This stylish home, where seven of the Carsons' eight children were born, became a popular visiting place for traders, dignitaries, and military men who wanted to meet the famous Kit Carson as they passed through New Mexico.

Owing to the region's mild climate, much of the Carson family's entertaining took place outdoors, and Carson's house, like many other adobes, came well equipped for such occasions with a rear patio shaded by a roof overhang and flanked by flower beds. Moreover, the patio oven could be used on warm days to keep cooking heat out of the home.

Carson and his wife occupied their adobe home for 25 years, though Kit was absent for long periods to scout for troops involved in the conquest of California, to conduct government business in Washington, D.C., and to fight Indians in Texas. Early in 1868, he moved his family to Boggsville, Colorado, but Josefa took ill in the spring and died due to complications from childbirth. A month later, suffering from a tumor on his trachea, Carson also died, at Fort Lyon, Colorado.

Following the Carsons' deaths, their Taos home was bought and sold several times, until in 1950 the Kit Carson Memorial Foundation acquired it, restored it, and worked to have it designated a National Historic Site. Some of Carson's furniture was recovered, and three of the home's rooms are now arranged as they were in the famed scout's time. The remaining rooms are set up as a museum, housing frontier artifacts from the region's Indian, Spanish, and American settlers. Today, visitors can tour Carson's home and his gravesite in nearby Kit Carson Memorial State Park. Also nearby is Carson National Forest.

Some of the furnishings in Carson's bedroom are original pieces, shipped to Taos from the Midwest over the Sante Fe Trail.

(Opposite) The Carsons' living room is furnished in Victorian style. Some of the furnishings are original to the home.

This 19th-century military desk, sits in the Carson living room. Kit would have had no use for the books and quill pen atop the desk; he was illiterate.

Eugene O'Neill

1888–1953

All these people I have written about, I once knew. I do not think you can write anything of value or understanding about the present. You can only write about life if it is far enough in the past.

From a letter to *The New York Times*

Photograph. c. 1920-21. Library of Congress.

EUGENE O'NEILL'S journey to Tao House, his home in Danville, California, from 1937 until 1944, was marked by great tragedy and great triumph. His father, James, was a successful touring actor who spent most of his days on the road. His mother became a morphine addict after his troublesome delivery in a New York hotel room in October 1888. His elder brother, Jamie, became a hopeless drunk. As a child, Eugene spent many nights in shabby hotel rooms and theater wings because his father did not want to spend money on comfortable lodging. Eventually the boy was sent to boarding school. He enrolled in Princeton but lasted only a short time, then left his family and spent several years drifting—prospecting in Honduras, working in Buenos Aires factories, and living the Bohemian life in New York City. During this period, he drank heavily, contracted malaria and tuberculosis, and attempted suicide.

The theater saved his life. After seeing the great plays of August Strindberg and Henrik Ibsen—and contrasting them with the melodramas in which his father performed—O'Neill began to write. After a few apprentice efforts, he wrote *Bound East for Cardiff*, a chilling sea drama that won praise for its realistic depiction of a sailor's life. The play gained him admission to a Harvard playwright's workshop in 1914, where he further honed his skills. In 1916, he joined a theater group in Provincetown, Massachusetts, and the troupe began performing his plays regularly. A short time later, the Provincetown Players moved to New York's Greenwich Village, where O'Neill's plays won critical acclaim. In the next ten years, he wrote over 25 plays and won three Pulitzer Prizes.

But O'Neill's personal life remained unsettled. His parents and older brother died, and two marriages failed. In 1929, he married an actress, Carlotta Monterey, and they settled in Georgia for several years, but the O'Neills disliked the climate and moved to California. In 1936, they bought a 158-acre estate on a high hill overlooking the San Ramon Valley and built Tao House.

Tao means "the right way" in Chinese, and O'Neill looked at his new hillside home partially surrounded by walls as a "final harbor" where he could settle down and work in peace. The L-shaped home, suggestive of a Spanish hacienda, was built with white basalite bricks to resemble adobe and topped with black Oriental tiles.

(*Opposite*) In 1936, Eugene O'Neill bought a 158-acre estate in Danville, California, where he built Tao House, an L-shaped home made of white basalite bricks and topped with black Oriental tiles.

The plain white stairway in the entrance hall is accented with theatrical masks from Japan.

The centerpiece of the music room is "Rosie," O'Neill's player piano.

Carlotta O'Neill's second-floor bedroom offers a spectacular view of the hills overlooking the San Ramon Valley.

Inside, the downstairs living quarters include a dining room, a living room, and a piano room, outfitted with a player piano called Rosie. The O'Neills' bedrooms are upstairs, as is Eugene's study, sheltered behind three doors and offering a spectacular view of the valley. The walls throughout the house are painted white, the ceilings blue, and the doors Chinese lacquer red. The north wing of the house, the bottom of the L, comprises the servants' quarters, kitchen, and service rooms. Completing the estate are gardens, a swimming pool, almond and walnut orchards, and several outbuildings.

In this tranquil setting, O'Neill wrote the plays that finally confront his tragic past— *A Moon for the Misbegotten*, *The Iceman Cometh*, and his masterwork, *Long Day's Journey into Night*, which, at his insistence, was not produced until after his death. In these gripping dramas that center on his family, O'Neill would "face my dead at last."

O'Neill sold Tao House in 1944 and moved East. In 1953, after enduring a degenerative nerve disease, one son's drug addiction, and another's suicide, he died in a Boston hotel room. Twenty years later, the Eugene O'Neill Foundation was formed to raise funds for the purchase of Tao House. In 1975, the foundation accomplished its goal, thanks in part to benefit performances of O'Neill plays by actor Jason Robards, one of the foremost interpreters of the playwright's tragic characters. In 1980, the estate was turned over to the U.S. government, and today Tao House is a National Historic Site managed by the National Park Service.

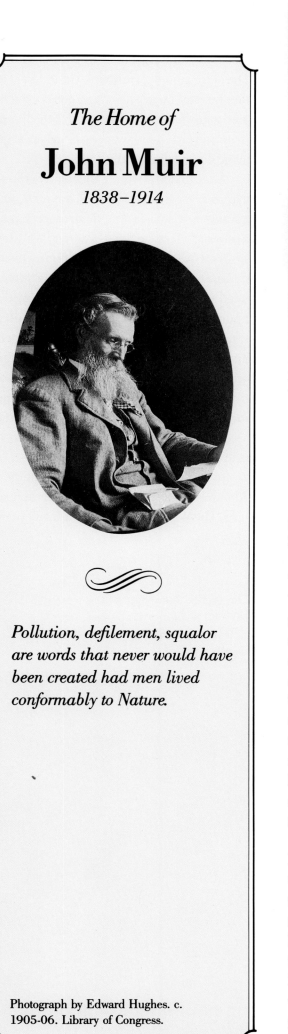

In 1890, John Muir and his family moved into this large Victorian home, topped by a bell tower, in Martinez, California.

MOST 19TH-CENTURY pioneers who settled the West wanted to tame the wilderness, but John Muir wanted to preserve it—as much of it as possible. Born in Scotland in 1838, he came to America at age 10 with his parents and settled on a farm in Wisconsin. After attending the University of Wisconsin, he traveled in Canada and lived for a time in Indianapolis where he worked in a machine shop. When an on-the-job accident caused permanent impairment of the sight in one eye, he quit, choosing instead to travel across the country, on foot, studying and marveling at nature's miracles—waterfalls, thick forests, wild flowers, awesome mountain ranges. He decided to devote his life to preserving the wilderness, which, in the decades after the Civil War, was rapidly beginning to disappear.

Early in 1868, after spending time in Florida and Cuba, Muir decided to explore the California mountains. When he first glimpsed the Sierra Nevadas, he knew he had found a new home. He bought a fruit ranch in the Alhambra Valley, where he made enough money to support his long hikes. In 1880, he married Louise Strentzel from Martinez and moved in with her parents. He also began to write to politicians and to other Americans involved in the budding conservationist movement, stressing the need to protect America's wilderness lands from further development.

In 1882, Mrs. Muir's parents acquired a new 17-room Victorian house down the road. When her father died, late in 1890, the Muirs and their two daughters moved into the home. To John's delight, the house had a front porch where he could sit and enjoy the aromas from his gardens and orchards. To add to his enjoyment, he planted large trees around the house.

Inside, a wide hallway connects five downstairs rooms—a family parlor with a large fireplace, a formal parlor, a library, a dining room, and a kitchen. On the second floor are several bedrooms and Muir's study housing his large collection of books. A stairway leads to attic rooms and to the bell tower in the rooftop cupola.

Muir spent the last 25 years of his life in this home. In his upstairs study he wrote the articles and books that rightfully took their place beside the works of Henry David Thoreau as some of America's finest nature writing. Muir's works helped make Yosemite Valley a National Park and led to the creation of the Sierra Club, which Muir served as president from its founding in 1892 until his death in 1914.

Today, the National Park Service administers John Muir's home as well as the adobe on the adjacent estate, which was once occupied by Muir's daughter and son-in-law.

Laura Ingalls Wilder

1867–1957

I wanted the children now to understand more about the beginnings of things, to know what is behind the things they see—what it is that made America as they know it.

From her speech during Bookweek, 1937

Photograph. 1891. Courtesy the Laura Ingalls Wilder Society. DeSmet. S.D.

LAURA INGALLS WILDER, the author of the *Little House* books that have entertained American children for more than 50 years, was born into a family of pioneers. Her father, Charles Ingalls, hailed from Cuba, New York, and moved west with his parents—first to Illinois, then to Wisconsin. The family of Laura's mother, Caroline Quiner, moved to Wisconsin from Connecticut. Laura was born near Pepin, Wisconsin, and spent the first 12 years of her life accompanying her parents on their many sojourns—to Missouri, Kansas, Minnesota, Iowa, and back to Minnesota. In 1879, Charles accepted a job as a timekeeper and paymaster at the Chicago & Northwestern Railway construction camp in De Smet, South Dakota, and the Ingallses moved again.

The family spent its first Dakota summer at the railway camp. In the fall of 1879, when the railroad surveying team departed, Charles arranged for his family to move into the surveyors' house for the winter. It was a large two-story structure, and the Ingallses' four daughters were delighted to have such spacious living quarters after the comparatively primitive conditions of the camp. The surveyors left food and supplies in the large downstairs pantry, so the family was set for the long Dakota winter. The older girls slept upstairs, Ma and Pa—as they became known in Laura's books—occupied a downstairs bedroom off of the living room and Grace, the youngest daughter, slept in the downstairs trundle bed.

After that first winter, the family moved into town. Soon stores, a school, a church, and homes were built around them as more pioneers settled in De Smet. Pa Ingalls built a store on Main Street, and the family lived there. For a time they also lived on a homestead south of town. Then in 1887, Pa Ingalls bought two lots on Third Street and built a small house that became the family's first permanent home. Later he added an ell to the original building, giving the structure a total of five first-floor rooms—living room, sitting room, kitchen, and two bedrooms—and three second-floor bedrooms. The house remained in the family until 1944.

In 1885, however, Laura had married Almanzo Wilder and left the Ingalls household. The Wilders moved to Florida five years

The Ingalls family spent the winter of 1879/80 at Surveyors' House, near the railroad construction camp where Pa Ingalls worked.

later, but returned to De Smet in 1892. Later they moved to Mansfield, Missouri. Laura's writing career began in 1911, when she sold her first article to the *Missouri Realist*. She soon became a columnist and editor of that newspaper and also began to sell her stories to national magazines. Her first book, *Little House in the Big Woods*, appeared in 1932; *Little House on the Prairie* was published three years later, the third of the nine *Little House* books that dealt with her childhood.

Laura continued writing until her death in 1957. Her *Little House* series was issued in paperback in 1971, and sales were spurred on by the NBC television series, *Little House on the Prairie*, which ran from 1974 to 1983.

Today, the surveyors' house where the Ingallses spent their first De Smet winter and the family home on Third Street are maintained by the Laura Ingalls Wilder Memorial Society. Each summer, *The Laura Ingalls Wilder Pageant*, an open-air play, is performed at the Ingalls homestead outside De Smet.

While the Ingallses lived at Surveyors' House, family activities centered on the stove in the large living room.

The Ingallses' home from 1887 through 1944 was this simple two-story house on Third Street in De Smet, South Dakota.

THE UNITED STATES has few castles. When the great medieval European fortresses were being built, America was essentially a vast unsettled wilderness. In 1919, however, William Randolph Hearst, head of the vast Hearst publishing empire, commissioned construction of a huge mansion on his 250,000-acre estate — called "La Cuesta Encantada" (Spanish for "Enchanted Hill") — on a high peak overlooking the village of San Simeon, California. The resulting building, which he called "La Casa Grande," became known quite simply as "Hearst's Castle."

William Randolph Hearst was the son of George Hearst, a Missourian who made a fortune during the great California gold rush. Like the children of many wealthy families of the Gilded Age, young William was sent to Harvard to acquire the finest education that America had to offer. But Hearst was expelled for pulling pranks, a great disappointment to his mother, who had supervised his early schooling. The university experience, however, was not a complete loss. While at Harvard, Hearst was the business manager of *Harvard Lampoon*, so after his expulsion he moved to New York to become a reporter with the *New York World* — at about the same time that his father purchased the *San Francisco Examiner*. In 1887, when the elder Hearst was elected to the U.S. Senate, he gave the newspaper, with great misgivings, to his son. At age 24, William had the beginning of a publishing empire that would eventually include more than 25 newspapers, 13 magazines, 8 radio stations, various wire services, and a couple of movie companies.

In 1919, when his mother died, William inherited the San Simeon estate, several silver mines, and a 1,000,000-acre California ranch. Tired of going to San Simeon and "camping in tents," Hearst hired Julia Morgan, a San Francisco architect trained in the French Beaux Arts style, to build a mansion on the estate, a magical kingdom where he could escape the pressures of the publishing world. She designed a 100-room castle in the Mediterranean Revival style, an imposing structure with red tile roofs and two cathedral-like towers rising 137 feet into the San Simeon sky.

(Opposite) In 1919, construction began on this 100-room castle on William Randolph Hearst's property in San Simeon, California.

The Greek temple facades flanking the Neptune pool gave swimmers the sense that they were guests on Mount Olympus.

For the next several years, the town's small harbor was filled with ships bearing marble, wood, and assorted art works from around the world. The project took more than 30 years.

La Casa Grande is 3½ stories high, not including a mezzanine between the first two floors. The first floor contains the public rooms — an assembly room off the front vestibule; a Gothic refectory which resembles a medieval dining hall; a morning room for breakfasting; a billiard room with Persian tiles, rugs, and art work; a theater; and a pantry. The second floor comprises a 90-foot-long library, with two attached study alcoves, and several bedrooms. The third floor holds Hearst's Gothic study, his bedroom, and several sitting rooms. The top floor has two bedrooms located in the large towers that front the house. Throughout the home, the staircases are small and unobtrusive, suggesting that each floor is a separate building.

La Casa Grande is surely the centerpiece of La Cuesta Encantada, but the surrounding grounds offer additional enchantments—

three large guest houses, called "Casa del Mar," "Casa del Monte," and "Casa del Sol"; indoor and outdoor swimming pools; temple facades; terraced gardens; and statues and balustrades that dot the grounds, reminding one of a Roman emperor's country villa. Hearst raised cattle and horses and imported zebras and other grazing animals to roam the vast acreage around the estate. He also created a private zoo, sheltering lions, bears, tigers, monkeys, and other species.

Work on La Cuesta Encantada continued during Hearst's lifetime; he planned numerous enhancements, including a great hall behind La Casa Grande. Even though he lived almost 90 years, he did not see his enchanted kingdom completed. He died in 1951, and several years later his family gave the home and part of the property to the State of California. Today, Hearst Castle is administered by the California Department of Parks and Recreation. Visitors can choose among four tours to view the house, outbuildings, and estate.

Hearst's third-floor study is furnished in the Gothic style.

176

The billiard room at Hearst's castle is accented with Persian paneling, rugs, and artwork.

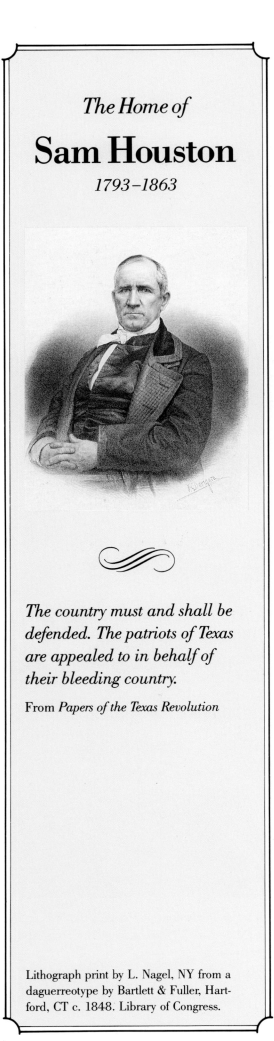
SAM HOUSTON is known to most Americans as the "Father of Texas Independence." Born in Virginia, raised in Tennessee, and adopted by the Cherokees, with whom he lived for several years, he went to Texas in 1832 as President Andrew Jackson's special envoy to the local Indian tribes. Within a few years, he had become involved in the struggle to free Texas from Mexican rule. He signed the Lone Star Republic's Declaration of Independence on March 2, 1836, and defeated the Mexican army in the decisive Battle of San Jacinto on April 21, 1836. That year he became the republic's first President, and he was Texas's first senator when it joined the United States in 1845.

After the Mexican War, Houston bought a small plantation named Ravenhill on the outskirts of Huntsville in the eastern part of the state. In 1848, he expanded his single-room cabin into Woodland Home, a six-room, two-story structure to accommodate his wife, mother-in-law, and children. The first floor features a wide central hallway—a "dog trot" in local parlance—that served as a dining room and sitting room. There is also a parlor and two bedrooms, while upstairs are two

Steamboat House, designed by Rufus Bailey to resemble a Mississippi River steamboat, was Houston's home from 1861 until his death two years later. The home, originally located in northern Huntsville, was moved to the Sam Houston Memorial Museum complex.

more bedrooms for the children. The house has front and rear porches and chimneys at each end. A replica of the kitchen and Houston's law office are housed in log cabins a short distance from the home.

Houston lived in Woodlawn Home until 1859, when he sold it to pay campaign debts. His political career came to an abrupt and painful end a few years later. As a senator he had opposed the popular Kansas–Nebraska Bill of 1854—which allowed slavery in certain western territories—because he believed it would lead to civil war. As a result, he lost the support of the Democratic Party. He still had sufficient popular appeal to be elected Governor of Texas in 1859, but after the outbreak of hostilities he was deposed by the military commanders in 1861 when he refused to take the oath of allegiance to the Confederacy. A man of high principles, Houston retired from public life.

When his governorship was terminated, he was unable to repurchase Woodland Home, so he rented Steamboat House, a rambling two-story home in northern Huntsville designed by Rufus Bailey to resemble a steamboat. The rectangular structure has a large front facade and is flanked on either side by long two-story porches that suggest the side railings on a Mississippi River steam-boat. Houston lived in Steamboat House until 1863 when he died in one of the front downstairs bedrooms.

During the 50 years after Houston's death, Woodland Home was sold several times, re-modeled, and moved. Sam Houston State Teachers College acquired the home in 1911 and began its restoration, though it did not regain its original appearance until several years ago. In 1936, the Sam Houston Memorial Museum was built a short distance from the home, and Steamboat House was moved to the Woodland estate. Today, the museum administers both Houston houses as well as his law office, a replica of the kitchen cabin, and a gift shop on the 15-acre piece of turf that the Father of Texas Independence called home.

This replica of Houston's original law office stands a short distance from Woodland Home.

Houston's parlor at Woodland Home features a handsome piano, a marble-top table, and other mid-19th-century furnishings.

179

Charles M. Russell

1864–1926

This was real picture country before boosters got ahold of it and made real estate out of it.

CHARLES MARION RUSSELL is known as one of the great artists of the American West, the master of frontier scenes who, according to Will Rogers, could "paint a horse and a cow and a cowboy and an Indian better than any man who ever lived." We might expect his residence to be a log cabin, adobe, or ranch house, but his neatly preserved home on Fourth Avenue North in Great Falls, Montana, in no way suggests the wild, wild West.

The two-story house with front and side gables and wraparound porch sits on a neat lawn and is surrounded by flowers and shrubs. Careful restoration—fresh paint, a new roof— make the home, built in 1900, appear newer than it is.

Inside, the front door leads to a foyer, entranceway, and four rooms—a living room, which originally served as Russell's studio, a dining room with built-in hutch, a kitchen, and a pantry. Throughout the house the plain plaster walls are accented with heavy wood molding. The second floor contains a sunroom, a master bedroom with sewing nook, and three other bedrooms. Charles and his wife, Nancy, had one child, Jack, whom they adopted after 20 years of marriage.

The house more closely reflects Nancy's tastes than Charles's. When Russell moved to Great Falls in the late 1890s, most of his cowboy experiences were behind him. He had left his native St. Louis as a teenager to work briefly as a sheepherder, and then as a night wrangler for 12 years. At age 32, he married 18-year-old Nancy Cooper of Cascade, Montana, and she convinced him to settle down in Great Falls and focus on what he had been doing only half seriously since his boyhood years: capturing the West in sketches and paintings. Nancy used money inherited from her mother's estate to buy a lot in a residential section of town and oversaw the construction of their pleasant house.

But the homestead has one symbol of Charles's cowboy days: the log cabin studio located a short distance from the house. In 1903, the Russells had a friend build Charles a small crib where he could paint in peace and privacy. Telephone poles were used to

In 1900, Charles M. Russell, the premier artist of the American West, built this modest two-story home in Great Falls, Montana. He lived here until his death in 1926.

construct the walls, and a large fireplace was installed where Charles could brew his cowboy stew. He used the cabin as a workroom and a place to entertain his old friends.

The Great Falls years were the most productive of his career. He painted, sculpted, and created illustrations for magazines; along the way, he became the highest paid artist of his era. In 1903, he went to New York for the first time to display his work, and the following year he held an exhibition at the St. Louis World's Fair. Numerous commissions followed, and today his paintings and sculptures are displayed in museums and galleries throughout the United States.

Russell died in 1926, at age 62. In 1929 Nancy sold the studio and cabin to the City of Great Falls. She died in 1941. For many years, the house was vacant and in disrepair. In 1971, however, the home and studio were restored by the Montana Federation of Garden Clubs, which still maintains the property. The two buildings and the nearby C. M. Russell Museum Complex, built in 1952, attract thousands of visitors a year who wish to view the work and home of one of America's most popular cowboy artists.

Charles died in this upstairs bedroom. The sun-filled sewing nook beyond the bed contains Nancy Russell's original sewing machine.

The Russells' living room features hardwood floors covered with decorative throw rugs, thick wooden ceiling beams, colorful wallpaper, and functional furniture. In Russell's day, the piano stood in the town's opera house.

181

The furnishings throughout the house reflect Nancy's contemporary tastes, but Charles' log cabin studio, located a short distance from the house, is right out of the Old West.

182

Sam Rayburn referred to the house on his ranch in Bonham, Texas, as "The Homeplace."

The Home of

Sam Rayburn

1882–1961

Give of yourself, give honestly. Take as little away as you can. Leave more behind than you take away.

Photograph. c. 1958. Courtesy the Sam Rayburn Home.

SAM RAYBURN was a member of the House of Representatives from 1913 to 1961 and Speaker of the House for all but four years between 1940 and 1961. He held that post—and was third in the line of succession for the presidency—longer than any other American. History buffs can get a good sense of the man and his political philosophy by visiting his home in Bonham, Texas. "The Homeplace," as Rayburn called it, is a modest two-story house which he built for his parents in 1916 on the 125-acre farm that they had purchased three years earlier. It is a simple, homey place for a man with simple tastes and homespun values.

Most visitors to Rayburn's home entered via the back porch. He had his office right inside the door, and he liked conducting business and receiving guests there. If there were too many visitors for the office, he brought them into the living room at the front of the house. Guests invited for dinner would eat in the pleasant family dining room and perhaps sleep in a first-floor guest room. When President Harry Truman visited Rayburn in Bonham, the dinner had to be served outside, because Mr. Sam—as his constituents called him—invited a thousand or so neighbors to meet the President. When the Secret Service expressed concern, Rayburn simply explained, "These are my friends. I know every man, woman, and child here. I'll vouch for them personally."

The Homeplace was also a home for Ray-

burn's parents, brothers, and sisters. At one time or another, three of Sam's siblings, a brother-in-law, and a cousin lived at the house. They used the six upstairs bedrooms; Sam slept in the biggest room when he was not in Washington. The house was remodeled twice over the years: an addition was erected in 1934 and a kitchen wing was added in 1940.

The Homeplace was not only a home, it was also a working dairy farm and cattle ranch. The smokehouse in the rear is still standing, as is the tractor shed, sheltering Sam's truck and his sister's 1957 Plymouth. Perhaps the only sign of pretentiousness can be found in the garage out back—Rayburn's 1947 Cadillac.

In Washington, Rayburn—Speaker of the House for 17 years, Democratic Majority Leader for several terms, chairman of the Democratic National Convention in 1948, 1952, and 1956—built a reputation as a man of impeccable integrity and bipartisan fairness who stood for the interests of farmers, small businessmen, and blue-collar workers. For decades he was one of Washington's most powerful men, but he never forgot his small-town roots, which may explain why his constituents elected him 24 times.

Rayburn died of cancer in 1961, at age 79, while still in office. In 1972, his family deeded the Bonham ranch to the State of Texas. Today, the estate is maintained by the Texas Historical Commission.

183

I want to see the temple built in a manner that it will endure through the Millennium.

From *Discourses of Brigham Young*

LIKE MANY OTHER 19th-century pioneers, Brigham Young made the dangerous pilgrimage west to find a new home, a fresh start on the open frontier. Unlike other settlers, however, Young left civilization not for gold or land but for peace — a place where he and his followers could practice their religion without interference.

Young was born in a log cabin on his family's farm in Vermont. When he was 14, his mother died and he left home to become an apprentice carpenter. He later moved to Mendon, New York, built a home for his wife and two daughters, and worked as a cabinet-maker, painter, and glazier. While living in New York, he chanced upon the Book of Mormon and was impressed with its teachings. He became a member of The Church of Jesus Christ of Latter-day Saints in 1832 and moved to Ohio shortly thereafter. He was named Apostle in 1835 in Kirkland, Ohio. In 1844, when Joseph Smith, the head of the Mormon Church in America, was murdered in Nauvoo, Illinois, Young became the new religious leader. Two years later, when persecution of his people became unbearable, Young led an exodus of 15,000 Mormons across the Midwestern prairie toward the Rocky Mountains. They settled near the Great Salt Lake in Utah and established a community where they could worship without persecution.

Seven years after the first Mormons reached Salt Lake City, after the settlers had overcome disease and starvation and had built adequate dwellings, Young commissioned the building of Beehive House as an official headquarters and home for the President of the Church. Young himself was a house builder by trade, but he called on Truman Angell, the architect who would later design the magnificent Salt Lake City Temple, to oversee the operation. Woodworkers, silversmiths, and stone cutters, as well as unskilled laborers all played their parts.

When Beehive House was completed, Young had as headquarters a building reminiscent of his native New England — a majestic 2½-story Greek Revival structure with a one-story columned porch (a second story was added later) and a splendid rooftop cupola surrounded by a balustraded terrace. The walls are made of sturdy adobe bricks, and the wood trim is made from timber cut in nearby forests. At the top of the cupola sits a white painted beehive, the Mormon symbol of industry. Woodwork and doorknobs throughout the house are embellished with the symbol.

Inside, the house is arranged to serve both

Young did most of his writing at this cherrywood secretary in his first-floor bedroom. On top of the desk are a brass inkstand and marble paperweight.

official and family functions. A wide entrance hall with thick carpeting and tasteful furnishings welcomes visitors. Off the hall is Young's bedroom and workroom, housing his mahogany bed and cherrywood desk. At the rear of the house is the formal dining room and the reception room remodeled to an octagonal configuration in 1888 by John Young. During Brigham Young's day, it was called the Men's Dining Room, and it served, not only as the dining hall for workmen but also as the setting for state dinners held for an impressive list of visitors — President Ulysses S. Grant, Jay Gould, Ralph Waldo Emerson, Mark Twain, and the like. The second-floor Long Hall with Victorian furniture shipped west in covered wagons was used to receive these visitors.

But the Beehive House was also a home for Young's family. An informal downstairs parlor with its piano, bookcases, and easy chairs was the center of family activity. The children's lives revolved around the second-floor schoolroom and playroom, and their mothers' activities were focused on the bustling kitchen, neatly arranged pantry, and large storage room. A cozy informal dining room was where the family ate supper. The family rooms are furnished with simple pieces, many designed and built by Young.

An impressive city grew around Beehive House. The Salt Lake Tabernacle was completed in 1867, and a college, later Brigham Young University, was established in 1875. The Temple, begun the same year as Beehive House, was finally dedicated in 1893, 16 years after Young's death.

Beehive House was extensively remodeled in 1888 and again a few years later. In 1959, however, the Mormon Church decided to restore the building to much of its condition in Young's day (while retaining some later additions). It was opened to the public in 1961.

In 1854, Mormon pioneers in Salt Lake City built Beehive House as a home and headquarters for their leader, Brigham Young.

The elegantly furnished Gardo Room at Beehive House was used for small formal receptions.

185

LUTHER BURBANK was a new Englander, born in Lancaster, Massachusetts, in 1849, who left his home soil at age 26 to live in the promised land of California. He had already earned a solid reputation in the field of horticulture by developing the long, fine-grained Burbank potato. As soon as he arrived on the west coast, he realized that he had settled in the best spot in the world to pursue his life's work: the development of new strains of fruit, flowers, and trees.

In 1877, Burbank started his first nursery — on rented land in Santa Rosa. His mother and sister joined him in California, and the family struggled for several years while Luther experimented with new budding and grafting techniques. His first big break occurred in 1881 when he developed a method of grafting buds from prune trees onto earlier-budding almond trees. Further experimentation led to the introduction of more than 100 varieties of hybridized plums. Soon a plum and prune industry was flourishing in Sonoma County, California, and Burbank was being hailed as the American "plant wizard."

In 1884, Burbank, enjoying the financial rewards of his discoveries, purchased a home on four acres of land on Santa Rosa Avenue. The modified Greek Revival house is modest in size; it has four first-floor rooms — a parlor, a music room, a dining room, and a kitchen — and three second-floor bedrooms. But the land surrounding the dwelling allowed Burbank to create some of the best gardens in California. He built a greenhouse a short distance from the residence, filled his acreage with large flower beds, and placed his hybrid trees around the estate. Next to his home, he planted a cedar of Lebanon that grew into a spectacular shade tree.

A year after he bought his new home, Burbank purchased 18 acres of land in nearby Sebastopol and established the Gold Ridge Farm, where he continued to develop new strains of trees and plants. The invention of the refrigerated railroad car and Burbank's own creative marketing techniques — he sent out catalogs advertising his trees, shrubs, and seeds to nurseries around the world — made him a small fortune. International fame followed. A contemporary of Thomas Edison

and Henry Ford, Burbank was seen as another American genius who helped bring the country into the modern age. Both men visited Burbank along with others, including naturalist John Burroughs and Helen Keller. Jack London, the author and Burbank's neighbor, consulted with the horticulturist while planning his own ranch.

Despite his splendid accomplishments, Burbank had many critics. Some botanists labeled his techniques as "unscientific." Moreover, religious fundamentalists denounced him because he used Charles Darwin's theory

of natural selection in developing his new strains of trees and plants. But criticism did not hamper Burbank; he passionately pursued his work even in his final years.

Burbank died in Santa Rosa in 1926, at age 77, and was buried near the cedar of Lebanon that he had planted years earlier. His wife, Elizabeth, 40 years his junior, bequeathed his home and property to the City of Santa Rosa upon her death in 1977. A second home built by Burbank in 1906, and his residence during the final two decades of his life, has been demolished.

Public tours of the home, greenhouse, and carriage house museum are offered spring through fall by the Luther Burbank Home & Gardens Board, which administers the Santa Rosa estate. Gardens filled with Burbank's Shasta daisies, pure-white Agapanthus lillies, bright-red tritomas, and contemporary hybrid roses surround the home. Many of Burbank's hybrid trees, planted almost a century ago, are still flourishing. The gardens are open daily year-round.

Burbank's home is surrounded by flower beds and gardens featuring the special strains that he developed during his remarkable career.

In 1884, Luther Burbank purchased this modest neoclassical home on a four-acre estate in Santa Rosa, California. One of Burbank's original greenhouses stands alongside the house.

(Above) This staircase, added to the home by Mrs. Burbank in the late 1920s, is made of Paradox walnut, developed by Luther in the 1880s.

(Left) The greenhouse office contains Burbank's original tools and worktable and a copy of his seed catalog.

ADDITIONAL INFORMATION

The Home of Henry Knox

New England

1 The Home of John Adams
(Peacefield), pp. 18–19
Adams National Historic Site
135 Adams Street
P.O. Box 531
Quincy, Massachusetts 02169
617-773-1177

2 The Birthplace of John F.
Kennedy, pp. 26–28
John F. Kennedy National Historic Site
83 Beals Street
Brookline, Massachusetts 02146
617-566-7937

3 The Home of Louisa May Alcott
(Orchard House), p. 29
Orchard House, Box 343
Concord, Massachusetts 01742
508-369-4118

4 The Home of Henry Knox
(Montpelier), pp. 24–25
Montpelier State Historic Site
P.O. Box 83
Thomaston, Maine 04861
207-354-8062

5 The Homes of Henry Wadsworth
Longfellow, pp. 30–31
a Longfellow National Historic Site
105 Brattle Street
Cambridge, Massachusetts 02138
617-876-4491

b The Wadsworth–Longfellow House
487 Congress Street
Portland, Maine 04101
207-772-1807

6 The Home of Herman Melville
(Arrowhead), pp. 20–21
Berkshire County Historical Society
780 Holmes Road
Pittsfield, Massachusetts 01201
413-442-1793

7 The Home of Paul Revere, pp. 36–38
19 North Square
Boston, Massachusetts 02113
617-523-2338

8 The Home of Harriet Beecher Stowe
(Nook Farm), pp. 40–41
The Stowe–Day Foundation
77 Forest Street
Hartford, Connecticut 06105
203-525-9317

9 The Birthplace of Gilbert Stuart, p. 17
815 Gilbert Stuart Road
Saunderstown, Rhode Island 02874
401-294-3001

10 The Homes of Mark Twain, pp. 14–16
a Mark Twain Memorial *(Nook Farm)*
77 Forest Street
Hartford, Connecticut 06105
203-525-9317

b The Mark Twain Home & Museum
(Boyhood Home)
208 Hill Street
Hannibal, Missouri 63401
314-221-9010

11 The Home of Cornelius Vanderbilt II
(The Breakers), pp. 32–33
The Preservation Society of Newport County
118 Mill Street
Newport, Rhode Island 02840
401-847-1000

12 The Birthplace of Daniel Webster, p. 39
Division of Parks & Recreation
P.O. Box 856
Concord, New Hampshire 03301
603-271-2343

13 The Home of Noah Webster, pp. 10–13
Noah Webster Foundation
227 S. Main Street
W. Hartford, Connecticut 06107
203-521-5362

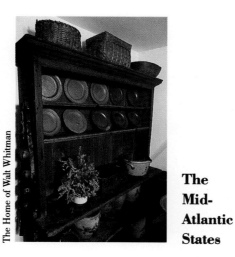

The Home of Walt Whitman

The Mid-Atlantic States

14 The Home of Susan B. Anthony, pp. 64–65
Susan B. Anthony Memorial, Inc.
17 Madison Street
Rochester, New York 14608
716-235-6124

15 The Home of Clara Barton, pp. 74–75
Clara Barton National Historic Site
5801 Oxford Road
Glen Echo, Maryland 20812
301-492-6246

16 The Home of Pearl S. Buck, p. 58
The Pearl S. Buck Foundation
Green Hills Farm, P.O. Box 181
Perkasie, Pennsylvania 18944-0100
215-249-0100

17 The Home of Frederick Edwin Church
(Olana), pp. 54–57
Olana State Historic Site
R.D. 2
Hudson, New York 12534
518-828-0135

18 The Homes of Thomas A.
Edison, pp. 59–61
a Thomas Edison National Historic Site
(Glenmont)
Main Street & Lakeside Avenue
West Orange, New Jersey 07052
201-736-5050

b The Birthplace of Thomas Edison
9 North Edison, Box 451
Milan, Ohio 44846
419-499-2135

c The Edison Winter Home
2350 MacGregor Boulevard
Ft. Myers, Florida 33901
813-334-3614

19 The Home of Washington Irving
(Sunnyside), p. 68
Historic Hudson Valley
150 White Plains Road
Tarrytown, New York 10591
914-631-8200

20 The Home of John Jay, pp. 62–63
John Jay Homestead State Historic Site
P.O. Box AH
Katonah, New York 10536
914-232-5651

21 The Homes of Edgar Allan Poe, p. 69
a Edgar Allan Poe House
203 N. Amity Street
Baltimore, Maryland 21223
301-396-7932

b The Edgar Allan Poe National Historic Site
532 N. Seventh Street
Philadelphia, Pennsylvania 19123
215-597-8780

22 The Homes of Franklin Delano Roosevelt
pp. 76–77
a Franklin Delano Roosevelt National Historic
Site *(Springwood)*
249 Albany Post Road
Hyde Park, New York 12538
914-229-9115

b Little White House Historic Site
P.O. Box 68
Warm Springs, Georgia 31830
404-655-3511

c Roosevelt Campobello International Park
P.O. Box 97
Lubec, Maine 04652
506-752-2922

23 The Homes of Theodore
Roosevelt, pp. 44–47
a Sagamore Hill National Historic Site
20 Sagamore Hill Road
Oyster Bay, New York 11771-1899
516-922-4447

b The Theodore Roosevelt Birthplace
28 E. 20th Street
New York, New York 10003
212-260-1616

24 The Home of Betsy Ross, pp. 51–53
239 Arch Street
Philadelphia, Pennsylvania 19106
215-627-5343

25 The Home of Frederick
Vanderbilt, pp. 70–73
Frederick Vanderbilt National Historic Site
249 Albany Post Road
Hyde Park, New York 12538
914-229-9115

26 The Homes of Walt Whitman, pp. 48–50
a Walt Whitman Birthplace Association
246 Old Walt Whitman Road
Huntington Station, New York 11746
516-427-5240

b Walt Whitman House
330 Mickle Boulevard
Camden, New Jersey 08103
609-964-5383

The Home of Marjorie Kinnan Rawlings

The South

The Home of George Rogers Clark

The Central States

The Home of Charles M. Russell

The West

PHOTO CREDITS

The Louise May Alcott Memorial Association, photos by M.L. Clarke 29

© Herbert K. Barnett 36-38

Berkshire County Historical Society 20-21
Biltmore Estate 108-111

© David Blankenship 55

© Alan Briere 6, 8-9, 10-13, 42-43, 44-53, 64-65, 75 (left column), 78-83, 85-87, 98-104, 114-117, 120-124, 132-141, 152-155, 189, 190 (left column), back cover (top row, 1st fr. l; 1st fr.r.; 2nd row, 2nd fr. l; 3rd row, 1st fr. r.; 4th row, 1st fr. r.)

The Pearl S. Buck Foundation 58

The Church of Jesus Christ of Latter Day Saints 184-185

The Henry Morrison Flagler Museum 2-3, 88-91

Joel Chandler Harris Association, Inc. 96-97

The President Benjamin Harrison Memorial Home 156-157

Hearst Monument/John Blades 174, 176-177

Historic Hudson Valley 68

Sam Houston Memorial Museum 178-179

Illinois Historic Preservation Agency/James D. Quick, photographer 150-151, back cover (4th row, 2nd fr. l.)

John Jay Homestead State Historic Site 62-63

Locust Grove 129-131, 190 (middle column)

Mount Vernon Ladies Association 119 (middle & bottom)

The National Park Service 18-19, 31, 59-60, 71-73, 74, 75 (top & right), 77, 106-107, 112-113, 171, back cover (2nd row, 3rd fr. l; bottom row l.)

Nebraska State Historical Society 126-128

The Preservation Society of Newport County/Richard Cheek 32-35

North Carolina Dept. of Cultural Resources/ Thomas Wolfe Memorial, courtesy of Nick Lanier 95

Friends of Olana, Inc., Olana State Historic Site 54, 56-57

Edgar Allan Poe House 69

© Radeka 142-144, 158-162, 164-170, 172-173, 180-182, 186-189, 191, 192, back cover (1st row, 2nd fr. l; 3rd row, l.)

Sam Rayburn House 183

The John & Mable Ringling Museum of Art 105

Will Rogers Birthplace 163

The Stowe-Day Foundation 40-41

SuperStock International 15 (bottom), 17, 22-25, 26-28, 30, 39, 61, 66-67, 70-71, 76, 84, 92-94, 118, 119 (top), 125, 145 (and front cover), 175

Mark Twain Memorial 14, 15 (top), 16

Frank Lloyd Wright Home and Studio Foundation /John Miller, Hedvich-Blessing 146-149

ACKNOWLEDGEMENTS

Grateful appreciation is made to the following individuals for their assistance in the creation of this book:

Adams National Historic Site, Caroline Keinath; Susan B. Anthony Memorial, Inc., Roberta Lachiusa; Arlington House, Agnes Mullins; Asociation for the Preservation of Virginia Antiquities, Nancy Packer; Clara Barton National Historic Site, Joe Burns, Joan Pryor, & Beth Hagler-Martin; Beauvoir, Keith Hardison; Berkshire Athenaeum, Ruth Deggehart; Berkshire County Historical Society at Arrowhead, Carolyn Banfield & Barbara Stoddard; Biltmore Estate, Sheri Jasiczek & Julie Betts; Daniel Boone Home, Gertrude Andrae; Molly Brown House, Dr. Ellen Fisher & Donna Jackson; Pearl S. Buck Foundation, Marie Miller & Mark Viggiano; Luther Burbank Home & Gardens, Kay Voliva; Kit Carson Foundation, Neil Poese; Church of Jesus Christ of Latter-Day Saints, Don LeFevre & Loni Manning; Buffalo Bill Cody Homestead, Dan Nagel; Buffalo Bill's Ranch State Historic Site, Tom Morrison; Frederick Douglass National Historic Site, Laurence Burgess, Bill Clark, & Carnell Poole; Thomas Edison Birthplace, Lawrence Russell; Thomas Edison National Historic Site, George Tselos & Joe Cravolta; Fair Lane, Henry Ford Estate, Donn Werling; Fairview, William Jennings Bryan House, Lynn Ireland; Henry Morrison Flagler Museum, Kay Graham; Florida Park Services, Alexandra Weiss; Friends of Montpelier, Edward O. Hahn; Ulysses S. Grant Birthplace, June Creager; Ulysses S. Grant Boyhood Home, Mary Ruffin; Ulysses S. Grant Home State Historic Site, Pete Campbell; Joel Chandler Harris Home, Karen Kelly; President Benjamin Harrison Memorial Home, Sue E. Small, Nick Perry, & Virginia Vezolles; Hearst Castle Monument, Shelley Scott & John Blades; Historic Hudson Valley, Laura Mogil; Sam Houston Memorial Museum, Samuel Angulo; Ivy Green, Helen Keller Birthplace, Sue Pilkerton; Jesse James Home; Gary Chilcote & Beth Grable; John Jay Homestead State Historic Site, Linda Connolly & Julia Wargar; John F. Kennedy National Historic Site, Sue Rigney & Leslie Obleschuk; Martin Luther King Historic District, Randolph Scott & Clark Moore; Ladies Hermitage Association, Edith Thonton & Sharon MacPherson; Library of Congress, George Hobbard; Abraham Lincoln Birthplace National Historic Site, Gary Tally; Abraham Lincoln National Historic Site, Gentry Davis, Kathey Dehart, & George Painter; Lindbergh National Historic Site, Charles Stone; Little White House Historic Site, Gretchen Terry; Locust Grove Historical Home, Gwynne Bryant & Cinda King; Longfellow National Historic Site, Bryan Doherty; Monticello, Millie Travis; Montepelier State Historic Site, Jan Howell; The Mount Vernon Ladies' Association of the Union, Christine Meadows & Karen Van Epps Peters; John Muir National Historic Site, Linda Stumpff & Phyllis Shaw; Museum of Fine Arts, Boston, Karen Otis; Ohio Division of Travel and Tourism, Linda More; National Park Service, Rick Lewis; Olana State Historic Site, James Ryan & Mrs. Eckerly; Eugene O'Neill National Historic Site, Craig Dorman & Julie Dreher; Orchard House, Jane Garden & Andi Perry; Edgar Allan Poe House, Jeff Jerome; Edgar Allan Poe National Historic Site, Richard Lahey; The Preservation Society of Newport County, Monique Panaggio; Marjorie Kinnan Rawlings State Historic Site, Sally Morrison; Sam Rayburn House, Dennis Chapman, & Carla Walker; Paul Revere House, Patrick Leehey & Gretchen Adams; The John & Mable Ringling Museum of Art, Pat Buck & Lucy Malone; Will Rogers Memorial Association, Greg Malak; Will Rogers State Historic Park, Barbara Rodriguez; Roosevelt–Vanderbilt National Historic Site, Duane Pearson, Beverly Kane, & Margaret Partridge; Sagamore Hill National Historic Site, Diane Dayson, Kathleen Young, Chris Merritt, & Ray Bloomer; Betsy Ross House, William Kingsley & Bill Carr; Rowan Oak, William Faulkner Home, Howard Bahr; C. M. Russell Museum Complex, Pam Yascavage; Aldred Scott; Stowe–Day Foundation, Laura Vassell, Earl French, & Marianne Curling; Gilbert Stuart Birthplace, William Geary; Taliesin West, Dixie Legler; Harry S Truman National Historic Site, Norman J. Reigle, & Palma Wilson-Buell; Tuskegee Institute National Historic Site, K. G. Jones; University of Florida – Rare Books Collection, Carmen Russell Hurff; Booker T. Washington National Monument, Alice Hanawalt; Daniel Webster Birthplace, Terry Edwards; Noah Webster Foundation, Sally Williams & Sally Whipple; Walt Whitman Birthplace Association, Barbara Bart; Laura Ingalls Wilder Home Association, Connie Tidwell; Laura Ingalls Wilder Society, Vivian Glover; Thomas Wolfe Memorial, Steve Hill; Frank Lloyd Wright Home & Studio Foundation, Arlene Sanderson.

The Home of Eugene O'Neill